To Alan

Xmas 1983

MARINE TROPICAL FISH IN COLOUR

Edited by Braz Walker

BLANDFORD PRESS

Published 1975 by Blandford Press Ltd
167 High Holborn, London WC1V 6PH
ISBN 0 7137 0723 2

 Adapted by Braz Walker from the original German text *Korallenfische im Aquarium* by Wilbert Neugebauer, published © 1973 by Franckh'sche Verlagshandlung, W. Keller and Co, Stuttgart.

Printed in Hong Kong   Bound in Great Britain

CONTENTS

INTRODUCTION

By Braz Walker

In the past, keeping marine aquarium fish was an impractical proposition for the average fishkeeper, unless he lived near the sea and could collect unlimited amounts of fresh sea water. Recent advances in aquarium design, the development of artificial salt mixes for the water, facilities and techniques for collecting, holding and transporting fishes, and the actual experience gained in the science of the marine aquarium have brought these fishes within the reach of any reasonably experienced and careful aquarist. To say that the keeping of marine fishes has reached a point of ease and convenience comparable with the keeping of freshwater species would be completely false and misleading. The fantastic beauty of the coral reef creatures, however, is worth the extra effort which you must necessarily expend. There literally is nothing like them.

Throughout this book there are references to fish anatomy in the color descriptions or physical descriptions of certain species. You can refer to the glossary of terms on page 17 for any explanation that you might need.

The Aquarium

Until a few years ago it was difficult to obtain an aquarium which was completely non-toxic when its cemented seams were exposed to the corrosive action of salt water. The first effective non-toxic models were made of Plexiglas and similar plastics, but these were not only expensive, they scratched very easily and often became unsightly in a short time. The advent of the "all-glass" aquarium did as much as anything to make marine fishkeeping practical.

The "all-glass" aquarium consists of five pieces of glass—two ends, a front, a back and a bottom—cemented together with silicone rubber cement. This cement is very strong and impervious to the action of salt water. It is semi-transparent, virtually unnoticeable, and leaves all the corners completely free of obstruction. Even when cured, it retains some of its elasticity, adding further durability against stresses which might be encountered from time to time. In some models, there may be a small piece of moulding around the top and bottom of the aquarium.

While the inner seams of older stainless steel-framed aquariums can be effectively covered with silicone rubber and made usable as marine tanks, it is recommended that all-glass aquariums be used instead. The prices are quite reasonable (often better than the more conventional stainless models), and not only are they more aesthetically pleasing, they are safe and non-corrosible both inside and out.

A marine fish aquarium should hold at least 20 gallons (75 litres)—the larger the better. Not only is a larger marine aquarium capable of initially supporting more fishes and other organisms, but the stability of the salt water is much greater than in a smaller tank. A stable environment is very important to the well-being of marine creatures of all kinds.

Water for the Marine Aquarium

Nothing is more basic for success in marine aquarium keeping then the quality of the salt water you use. You must consider two factors when thinking of water quality: the initial ability of the salt water to support marine life; the continuing ability of the medium to supply and maintain the needs of the fishes and other creatures during the subsequent, constant biological changes that take place within the aquarium.

Since marine creatures live in natural sea water it would seem logical that this would be the ideal medium in which to keep them. Sea water is a tremendously complex compound containing the most abundant, as well as the rarest, of earth's elements. Some of these elements are in water soluble compounds, such as salt and epsom salt, while others are found in almost infinitesimal quantities. These last are known as "trace elements", and they are often quite essential to the maintenance of marine life. Natural sea water obviously has all of the trace elements. It can, however, contain other less desirable substances, especially if improperly collected and prepared for use.

If natural sea water is to be used, it should be collected on a calm day far enough out at sea to be completely free of any turbidity caused by wind or wave action. It should also be collected away from areas of possible pollution. Collect and store it in non-toxic receptacles, such as plastic containers. No matter how pure and clear it appears, natural water contains living organisms. Therefore, you must seal and store it for at least three weeks in order to let it stabilize. This is best accomplished in relative darkness or by using light-free containers.

For most amateur aquarium situations, a number of excellent marine salt mixes are available which are better in several ways than natural sea water. Although synthetic water does not contain all the trace elements found in natural sea water, it contains those essential to the support of marine life. Storage is simplified since the salt can be mixed with tap water shortly before it is needed. Also, because there are no living organisms present, it does not require "ageing" to stabilize it, and it is free of the possibility of pollution, since tap water is perfectly suitable for most brands.

Most synthetic sea salts are prepackaged to mix with various given amounts of tap water. Instructions are provided on the package and should be followed carefully since they may vary in the number of steps or in sequence. Mix the water away from the aquarium and gently aerate it at least one night before using. Plastic containers with lids or caps are again useful; garbage cans of 20 or 30 gallons (75 or 110 litres) are available which serve very well. It is also a good idea to prepare some water ahead of time for replacement or for emergencies.

Salinity

Whether you use natural or artificial sea water, the salt content or salinity must be maintained at the correct level. This is easily measured with an inexpensive hydrometer which can be obtained from your fish dealer. The hydrometer measures the *specific gravity* of the water in relation to distilled water. In other words, the more salt dissolved, the heavier the water. Distilled water has a specific gravity of 1.000, normal sea water around 1.025. The hydrometer (which has a scale of graduations on it) simply floats higher in the heavier sea water.

The specific gravity of the water will vary slightly with the temperature, but if the water is maintained near 1.024 plus or minus 1 point (1.023 to 1.025), at a temperature of 21 to 24°C. (70 to

75°F.) it should be within the range easily tolerated by even delicate animals. For sturdier species, the reading can vary 2 points either way without harm, although it is much better to adhere as closely as possible to the median value.

Proper pH Level

The term pH is used for expressing the relative acidity or alkalinity of the water, based on a scale of 0 to 14, with 7.0 representing the neutral point. Any reading below 7.0 (for instance, pH 6.4) is more acid, while anything above 7.0 (such as pH 7.4), is more alkaline. Simple test kits are available for determining the pH levels, and every serious marine aquarist should have one and use it regularly.

Normal marine water or sea water should have a pH of about 8.3, which by fresh-water standards is rather alkaline. While less alkaline water is acceptable, marine creatures require water which remains on the alkaline side for good health. An acceptable range of between 7.5 and 8.3 can be maintained ordinarily if the substrate is composed of gravel high in calcium (such as crushed coral or dolomite), and if the aquarium is not overcrowded. The calcium carbonate contained in the gravel dissolves slowly in the water, which results in maintaining an alkaline condition.

Ammonia, Nitrite and Nitrate Levels

In a closed marine system there is no way to avoid the presence of ammonia, nitrite and nitrate, all of which are by-products of the functions of the living creatures. Excessive amounts can be toxic, so it is highly important to keep their concentrations below the levels at which they become detrimental. The key to this is good aquarium maintenance: not overcrowding, not overfeeding, and changing part of the water on a regular basis. Dead animals and uneaten food must be removed immediately.

Ammonia is the most toxic of these three chemicals and should be kept to less than .01 ppm (part per million). Nitrite and nitrate levels should remain below 0.1 ppm and 20.0 ppm respectively. Test kits are available for determining these levels and it is recommended that readings be taken regularly, especially in aquariums containing sensitive species. Particularly sensitive fishes are pointed out in the catalogue section of this book.

Filtration

Filtration in the marine aquarium serves much the same purpose as in the fresh-water aquarium, but is of much greater importance. Not only does filtration help keep the water clear, but proper filtration also helps keep the water in prime condition for a longer period of time.

Two types of filtration are ordinarily used in marine aquariums: biological and mechanical.

The most commonly used biological filtration system is the undergravel filter, which consists of a perforated plate covering the bottom of the aquarium which is itself covered by the aquarium substrate or sand. By connecting an air supply to airlift tubes on the filter, water is drawn through the substrate and the filter plate and returned to the aquarium. Waste products are also drawn into the substrate. Natural bacterial colonies soon form which consume the waste and convert it to harmless by-products. During this natural process, ammonia and other compounds are formed which can become toxic if their levels become too high. If you carefully avoid overfeeding and overcrowding and regularly replace a portion of the water, this situation is less likely to occur.

In mechanical filtration, solid waste is drawn through a filter medium such as polyester fibre or charcoal or a combination of both. When the medium becomes loaded, it is either cleaned or replaced. Fibre wool is an efficient remover of solid waste. Charcoal or, better yet, activated carbon, effectively absorb quantities of undesirable gases and other products.

An "outside filter" containing both wool and charcoal or carbon is recommended. This consists of a box which contains the filter material and hangs on the outside rim of the tank. Water enters the box through a siphon and is returned either through an airlift or motor-driven pump. This is known as a "power filter" and is very efficient. It is self-contained, while undergravel filters and non-power filters require a separate air supply to power them.

A combination of undergravel filtration and outside filtration is recommended.

Heating

Just as for fresh-water aquariums containing tropical fishes, the marine aquarium should be supplied with a heater if the room temperature is subject to fluctuations. There are numerous styles, wattages and price ranges of aquarium heaters. A good rule is 2 to 5 watts of power per gallon (3.8 litres) of water. A 2-watt-per-gallon heater is adequate for most situations which are not likely to be subject to extreme cold. Most marine fishes do well at a temperature of 21 to 24°C. (70 to 75°F.).

The heater should have an outside adjustment knob, preferably with a cap to cover it and keep water from splashing on top and running in or round the control or wiring insert. This is more important than with heaters for fresh-water tanks, since salt water is extremely corrosive.

Don't skimp on the price of the heater. Buy one of the highest quality and you will be assured of its safety, longevity and reliability.

Lighting

While nothing is comparable to natural lighting, few modern aquarists deny themselves the convenience and control of artificial aquarium reflectors. The fixtures inside the reflector can be either incandescent or fluorescent. Some aquarists prefer the former for its basic economy and the way it shows up the colors, while others prefer the latter for the coolness of its light, the much greater life of the bulbs, and the even nature of its light distribution. Fluorescent lighting seems more desirable on an all-round comparative basis. Either type should be provided with a glass guard beneath the light to protect against accidental splashing and corrosion.

The aquarium should remain covered to keep the fish in, undesirable substances out, and evaporation low. A "full cover" aquarium hood is good for these purposes.

Feeding Marine Fishes

Proper nutrition is essential to the well-being of marine fishes. While most fresh-water fishes will accept and do reasonably well on commercially prepared foods, most marine species will not thrive on such limited fare, and many will simply find it unacceptable. Available, however, are commercially prepared foods especially formulated for marine fishes. These are quite satisfactory for those fishes which will accept such preparations, but they should be supplemented with other foods.

FROZEN FISH or FROZEN SHRIMP are standard fare for many marine fishes. Frozen fillets available at fish markets are excellent and convenient. Flounder, halibut and similar fish are best. Oily types should be avoided. Shrimp should be frozen, uncooked table shrimp.

For feeding either shrimp or fish, cut off a piece while it is still frozen and return the remainder to the freezer. When partially thawed, cut the fish or shrimp into bite-sized pieces which can be easily handled by the various fishes. For small-mouthed fishes such as Butterflies you must chop it rather fine. On the other hand, fish such as Groupers have the ability to swallow quite large pieces of food.

FROZEN ADULT BRINE SHRIMP are readily eaten by many fishes, but should be supplemented with other foods.

LIVE BRINE SHRIMP are excellent for enticing stubborn individuals to eat. Newly hatched brine shrimp, called "nauplii", are hatched from dried eggs obtained from your dealer. This is a very good food for small fishes. Since nauplii are hatched in salt water, they will live in the aquarium until eaten. All newly hatched shrimp must be carefully separated from the shells before feeding. Live adult brine shrimp are available from some dealers, and some aquarists raise them to adulthood (about 5 mm or $\frac{3}{16}$ inch), just bite-size for many fishes.

Other live foods such as earthworms, white worms, Grindal worms, so-called "bloodworms" (which are actually the larvae of gnats or midges of the family Tendipedae) and mosquito larvae are also very good.

There are new frozen food products becoming increasingly available, including chopped clam, squid, plankton and algae which will continue to make the feeding of marine fishes easier.

Plant food is essential for keeping certain fishes such as Tangs or Surgeon Fishes and Butterflies. Frozen spinach is good. Lighting will help supply some natural algae if the aquarium is situated in a bright location. Sunlight, for this reason, is beneficial, although direct sunshine should be avoided. Algae can also be grown in a separate all-glass container of marine water.

You should feed marine fishes at least twice per day. They must not be overfed, since uneaten food will quickly pollute the water and raise the ammonia level intolerably high. Offer food in small amounts, letting these small portions be completely consumed before offering more. As soon as the fish begin to be satisfied, stop feeding them and remove any uneaten food from the tank.

Health and Diseases

Careful selection of healthy fishes is of utmost importance when purchasing marine fishes. Never buy fishes whose flanks are sunken or in which the fleshy area just below the dorsal fin is even slightly concave, instead of plump and convex as it should be. (This will be less obvious in some fishes than in others.) Also, avoid fishes with hollow bellies, skin blemishes or discoloration, cloudy or clamped fins, except, of course, in the few cases where one of these descriptive items is a characteristic of the species.

Try to observe fishes you wish to buy at feeding time and buy those which feed well and seem most alert. If possible, buy fishes which the dealer has had for a couple of weeks and which seem to be well acclimatized.

As with fresh-water fishes, there are marine fish diseases which occasionally present problems. You can get handbooks on marine aquarium maintenance describing the most common of these diseases and their cures. Your fish dealer may also help with suggestions or remedies.

Try to obtain healthy fishes and give them good care. That is the best prevention.

GLOSSARY

ANAL FIN: The single fin found just behind the vent. It may consist of soft rays or may contain a few anterior spines.

ANUS: The vent.

BARBELS: Sensory appendages or "whiskers" typically found on catfishes.

Caudal Fin: The tail.

Dorsal Fin: The fin located on the upper back. There can be either one or two dorsal fins, consisting of spines, soft rays or both.

Indo-Pacific Region: The area of the oceans surrounding Malaysia, Indonesia and that latitude of the Pacific Ocean.

Lateral Line: A line found on the sides of many fishes, consisting of one or more canals containing cutaneous (skin-imbedded) sensory cells. In many fishes it looks as if it had been scored by the point of a very sharp knife.

Operculum: The gill cover.

Pectoral Fins: The breast fins, usually found on the sides just behind the gill openings. They are paired.

Pelvic Fins: The ventral fins.

Soft Rays: Fin rays without spines. They may be either branched or unbranched.

Spines: Fin rays which are stiff and bony. They are capable of puncturing the flesh.

Vent: The excretory opening found on the underside of the fish.

Ventral Fins: Paired fins usually found on the underside of the fish just in advance of the vent. The fin rays may be either soft or spiny.

GENERAL MARINE FISH GROUPS

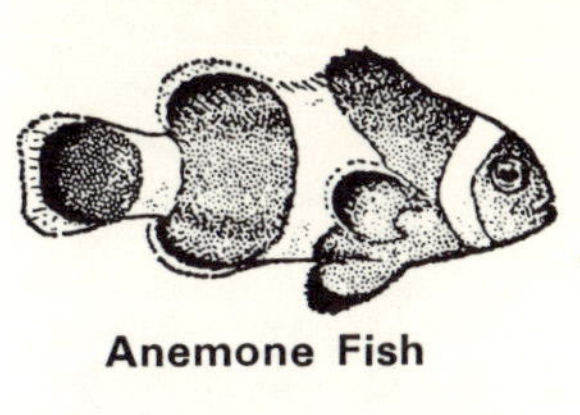

Anemone Fish

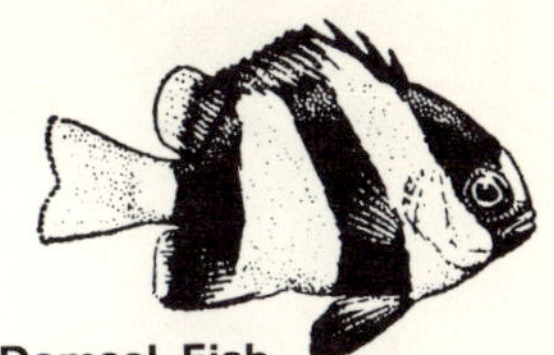

Damsel Fish

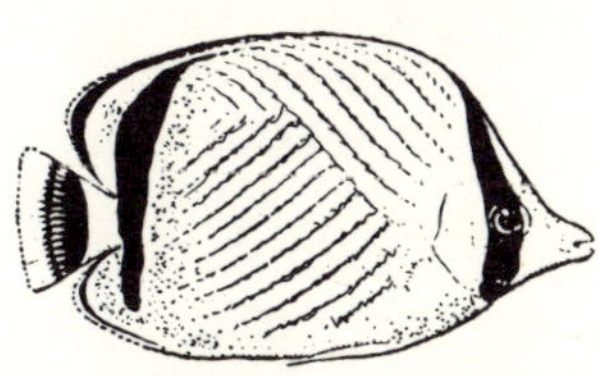

Butterfly Fish

Angelfish

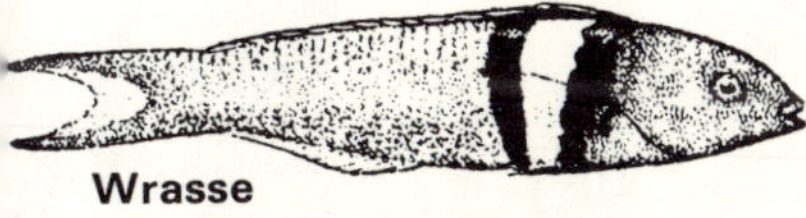

Wrasse

Cleaner Fish

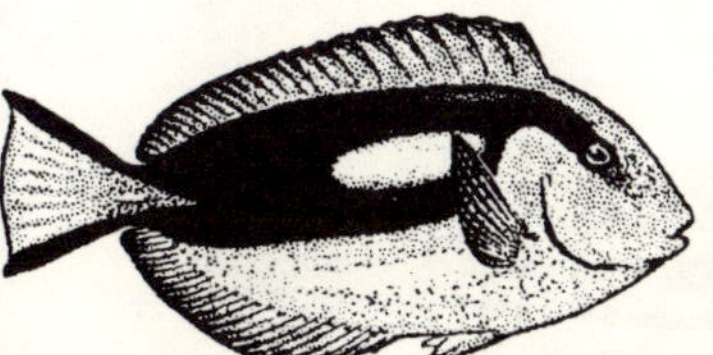

Surgeon Fish

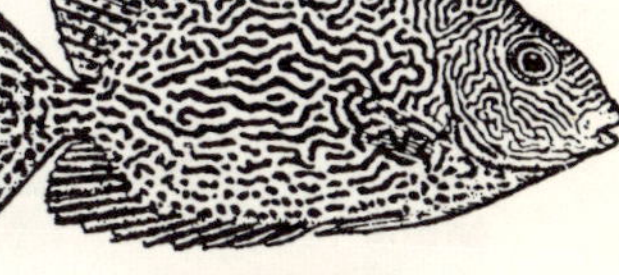

Rabbit Fish

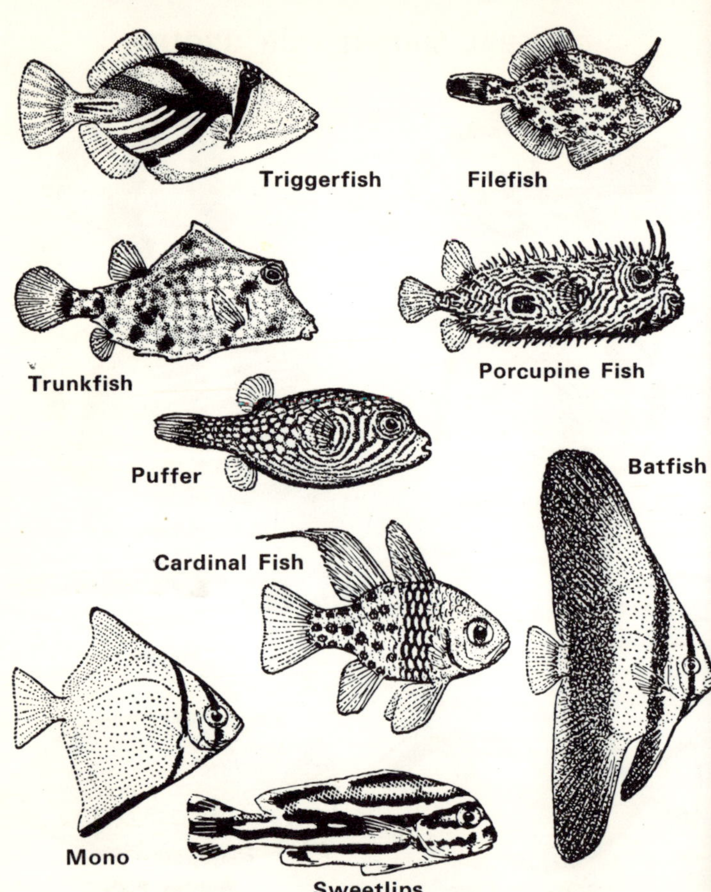
Triggerfish
Filefish
Trunkfish
Porcupine Fish
Puffer
Batfish
Cardinal Fish
Mono
Sweetlips

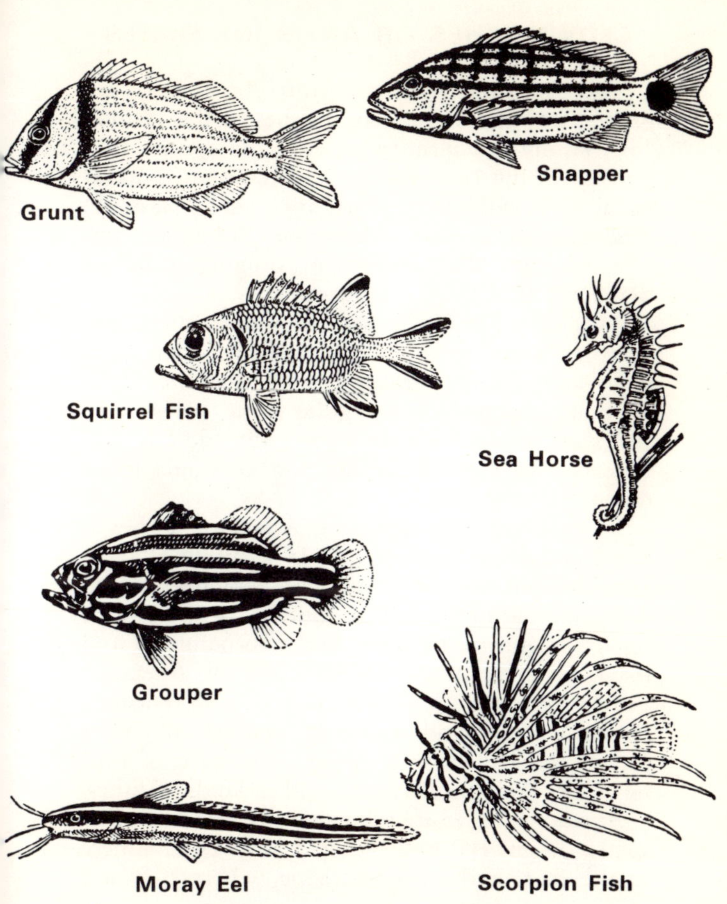
Grunt
Snapper
Squirrel Fish
Sea Horse
Grouper
Moray Eel
Scorpion Fish

CLOWNFISHES OR ANEMONE FISHES

The Anemone Fishes (genus *Amphiprion*) are among the best known coral fishes of the Damsel Fish family (Pomacentridae). Of the species that flourish in the Indo-Pacific region, about a dozen usually live with the large sea anemones (*Stoichactis, Radianthus, Discosoma*). Anemone Fishes are unaffected by the nettle-like stinging cells or nematocysts of the sea anemones.

Anemone Fishes do best in well-aerated, uncrowded aquariums. The water should have a pH of at least 7.6, preferably higher, and should be partially changed on a regular basis, perhaps 10 per cent every 2 weeks. Good filtration is also necessary to keep the nitrite and ammonia levels down.

Be sure the food you feed Anemone Fishes is small and diversified enough. In addition, if at all possible, put in the tank sea anemones (which demand marine water of the first quality with regard to purity, freshness and non-pollution and like strong lighting). Adult pairs of Anemone Fishes take over a sea anemone for living quarters, which they defend valiantly against all other members of their own species. In spite of this, however, they hardly bother other kinds of fishes.

Anemone Fishes are relatively easy to breed. The spawn, about 100 to 200 rather large eggs, adhere to the foot of the sea anemone, where they are protected by the tentacles. After about 10 days, the eggs hatch into proportionately husky fry. For the first 8 to 10 days, the fry must be fed extremely fine plankton (for example, *Euplotes*). Later on, they are ready to eat newly hatched *Artemia* or brine shrimp.

FAMILY: Pomacentridae.
SCIENTIFIC NAME: *Amphiprion akallopisos* Bleeker.
POPULAR NAME: **Skunk-striped Anemone Fish; White-backed Clownfish.**

Skunk-striped Anemone Fish

DISTRIBUTION: Tropical reaches of the Indian and Pacific Oceans; widespread but not numerous.
HABITAT: Reef and lagoon areas where its primary host, *Radianthus ritteri*, is found.
DESCRIPTION: The body is orange with light tan fins. There is a white mid-dorsal stripe and the basal portion of the dorsal fin is also whitish. A smaller species; not very aggressive. Easily acclimatized and very hardy.
LENGTH: To 8 cm (about 3⅛ inches).
COMMENT: Accepts various sea anemones. As with other fishes of the family, anemones are not a necessity, but they add a pleasing quality to the aquarium.

FAMILY: Pomacentridae.
SCIENTIFIC NAME: *Amphiprion frenatus* Brevoort.
POPULAR NAME: **Tomato Clown.**
DISTRIBUTION: A large part of the Indian Ocean and the western Pacific Ocean.
HABITAT: Coral reefs.
DESCRIPTION: Bright brick red or darker. When young, has two cross-stripes, of which only the first one, if any, lasts into adulthood.
LENGTH: 10 to 12 cm (4 to 4¾ inches).
COMMENT: A very sturdy species that is rather easy to breed. Spawns on sea anemones, such as *Actinia equina*.

Tomato Clown

FAMILY: Pomacentridae.

SCIENTIFIC NAME: *Amphiprion percula* (Lacépède).

POPULAR NAME: **Clown Anemone Fish; Orange Anemone Fish; Orange Clownfish; Percula Clownfish.**

DISTRIBUTION: Indian Ocean, Indonesian-Australian Archipelago and the western Pacific Ocean.

HABITAT: Reef and lagoon areas. As with other *Amphiprion* species, *A. percula* is never found more than a few metres from its host actinarian (anemone).

DESCRIPTION: The body, head and fins are brownish to bright orange, sometimes interspersed with black. The bars and fin margins are white with black borders. This is the smallest species of the genus. Frequently imported. Fresh imports especially sensitive; even after some time in the aquarium, they are more sensitive than most other species.

LENGTH: To 10 cm (4 inches).

COMMENT: A large *Actinia* sea anemone can be populated by a number of pairs. Although the fish-anemone relationship is pleasing, anemones are not necessary to the well-being of this or other Anemone Fishes. Buy only healthy, alert, finned fish which are feeding well and have no signs of disease. Not recommended for the beginner.

Clown Anemone Fish

FAMILY: Pomacentridae.
SCIENTIFIC NAME: *Amphiprion polymnus* (Linnaeus).
POPULAR NAME: **Saddle-backed Clownfish; Saddle-spotted Anemone Fish.**
DISTRIBUTION: Coasts of Indonesia and the western Pacific Oceans. Hub is in the Philippines.
HABITAT: Reef areas.
DESCRIPTION: The body is dark reddish brown; the face is lighter. There is a white band behind the eye, a post dorsal white saddle-spot, and a white caudal border. Quite uncommon.
LENGTH: 12 to 14 cm ($4\frac{3}{4}$ to $5\frac{1}{2}$ inches).
CARE: In spite of its beauty, but on account of the difficulty in keeping, not recommended for the home aquarium.
COMMENT: This species is very sensitive and seldom imported.

Other quite hardy *Amphiprion* species are the black-and-white-banded *Amphiprion xanthurus, A. sebae, A. bicinctus* and *A. melanopus. Amphiprion perideraion* is delicate.

Saddle-backed Clownfish

DAMSEL FISHES

Along with Anemone Fishes, many Damsel Fishes are highly suitable "beginner fish" for the marine aquarium. They are sturdy, modest in their demands of water quality and food, and are not as aggressive as many species of the closely related *Pomacentrus* and others.

These small-mouthed plankton eaters often live in sea anemones or among coral stems while young. They do not stray far from their habitat, so they can retreat into safety with lightning swiftness when danger threatens. In attack and defence, they make loud, clicking sounds.

Adults usually live together in pairs and spawn frequently in the aquarium—as often as three times a month. The spawning place is cleaned by the male. A large number of eggs—10,000 to 30,000—are laid. The eggs are attached by stalks to flat surfaces, such as stones, stone coral and fan coral, and are guarded until they hatch. The fry that hatch out after a few days are so tiny that the number composing the brood can scarcely be counted.

Because Damsel Fishes are sociable and easy to keep and breed, they are frequently found in aquariums. In order to derive the most pleasure from them, however, acquire several of the species. Also, provide a number of hiding places for them when constructing their living quarters, and see to it that they have a wide variety of nourishing foods such as live or frozen brine shrimp, chopped fish and shrimp (fresh or frozen).

FAMILY: Pomacentridae.
SCIENTIFIC NAME: *Dascyllus aruanus* (Linnaeus).
POPULAR NAME: **Three-striped Damsel Fish; White-tailed Damsel Fish.**
DISTRIBUTION: Widespread in the Indo-Pacific region.
HABITAT: Reef areas.

Three-striped Damsel Fish

DESCRIPTION: The white ground of the body darkens somewhat at night; fish that are dark in the daytime do not feel well. A white forehead spot appears only on the smaller female. Very hardy. Frequently imported.
LENGTH: To 9 cm ($3\frac{1}{2}$ inches).
CARE: Like all other *Dascyllus* species, it should be kept in small groups. It is a territorial species, however, and should therefore be provided with plenty of space and ample swimming room. It is not sensitive regarding food, and will even accept freeze-dried food.
COMMENT: This fish is very similar in appearance to *Dascyllus melanurus*, whose caudal fin is black instead of white (*melanurus* means "black tail").

Other *Dascyllus* which behave similarly are: *D. melanurus*, *D. arcuatus* and *D. marginatus*.

FAMILY: Pomacentridae.
SCIENTIFIC NAME: *Dascyllus carneus*.
POPULAR NAME: **White-tailed Damsel Fish.**
DISTRIBUTION: Indian Ocean and the western Pacific.
HABITAT: Reef areas.
DESCRIPTION: The head and throat areas are grey, the body lighter, each scale having a bluish streak. The ventral, anal and upper dorsal fins are dark to black. A darkish band runs from the anterior

White-tailed Damsel Fish

dorsal rays through the pectorals. The white spot on the shoulder helps gauge the health of this species: when the fish is sick, the spot disappears.
LENGTH: Up to 9 cm (3½ inches), but usually smaller.
COMMENT: This species, like other *Dascyllus*, is hardy and not difficult to care for, but is also rather aggressive. This fish appears to be closely related to *Dascyllus marginatus* and *D. reticulatus*.

FAMILY: Pomacentridae.
SCIENTIFIC NAME: *Dascyllus reticulatus* (Richardson).
POPULAR NAME: **Reticulated Damsel Fish.**
DISTRIBUTION: A wide part of the Indian and Pacific Oceans.
HABITAT: Frequently found among staghorn coral growth.
DESCRIPTION: Dark reddish-brown head. The body has a dark band from the anterior dorsal edge to the belly, with whitish sides darkening towards the ends of the anal and caudal fins. The spinous dorsal fin is dark to black. The dark edges of the scales are responsible for the appearance of reticulation. Regularly imported.
LENGTH: To 8 cm ($3\frac{1}{8}$ inches).
COMMENT: This species spawns on staghorn coral in nature. The male prepares the spawning site and assumes guard over the eggs until hatching.

Reticulated Damsel Fish

Three-spot Damsel Fish

FAMILY: Pomacentridae.
SCIENTIFIC NAME: *Dascyllus trimaculatus* (Rüppell).
POPULAR NAME: **Three-spot Damsel Fish.**
DISTRIBUTION: Widespread in the Indo-Pacific region and the Red Sea.
HABITAT: Found in small schools around coral reef heads.
DESCRIPTION: Entirely black, including the fins, with a white frontal spot and another white spot on each side just below the dorsal fin. These spots, if very white, indicate that the fish is in good health. During the spawning period, the black lightens to a reddish grey. This is the most frequently imported species of its genus.
LENGTH: 12 to 15 cm ($4\frac{3}{4}$ to 6 inches).
CARE: Should not be kept alone, but easily bred and not very aggressive. Feeds in nature on copepods, shrimp and crab larvae.
COMMENT: *Dascyllus albisella*, which replaces this species in Hawaii, is very similar, but the subdorsal spot is much larger and extends further down the body.

OTHER DAMSEL FISHES

In addition to the Anemone Fishes (genus *Amphiprion*) and the Damsel Fishes of the genus *Dascyllus*, other genera of the large pomacentrid family are also imported, such as *Pomacentrus, Chromis, Abudefduf*, and others. As a rule, these are all hardy and easy to care for. The disadvantage in keeping these vibrant and lively little fishes is their aggressiveness. As fry, they live mostly in schools in thick growths of coral, but as they grow older, they become more and more aggressive loners, and also lose the gleaming coloration of their youth.

Keeping these fishes is easier in large tanks that are systematically arranged. Take care, however, in choosing species, and watch adolescent fishes carefully, for they are prone to attack one another suddenly.

Some members of the genus *Chromis* are rather peaceful (for example: *C. caeruleus, C. xanthurus, C. dimidiatus* and *C. marginatus*). Of the *Abudefduf* species, *A. saxatilis, A. sexfasciatus, A. leucogaster, A. parasema* and *A. assimilis* are also more peaceful. *Pomacentrus* species are mostly quarrelsome loners which, in spite of being easy to care for, are not recommended.

Blue Damsel Fish; Blue Devil

FAMILY: Pomacentridae.
SCIENTIFIC NAME: *Abudefduf assimilis* (Bleeker).
POPULAR NAME: **Blue Damsel Fish; Blue Devil; Blue Maiden; Sapphire Reef Perch.**
DISTRIBUTION: The Philippines and the western Pacific Ocean.
HABITAT: Reef areas.
DESCRIPTION: Gleaming sky blue, in both young and adult forms. In the male, the fins and body are blue, the caudal and anal fins sprinkled with black. The female is lighter and the caudal fin is without coloration. Frequent in Philippine imports.
LENGTH: To 8 cm ($3\frac{1}{8}$ inches).
CARE: Easy to care for in a small school. Males are aggressive towards each other. For this reason, as

with all other related species, be sure the aquarium has many good hiding places.

COMMENT: Coloration is an indicator of the fish's health: it turns dull to dirty grey when it is sick, frightened, or in the wrong environment. This hardy fish is one of the more readily available and often among the less expensive of marine exotics. Few fishes have more breathtaking coloration than the Blue Devil, which is, unfortunately, because of its aggressiveness, rather deserving of its name.

FAMILY: Pomacentridae.
SCIENTIFIC NAME: *Abudefduf oxyodon* (Bleeker).
POPULAR NAME: **Emerald Perch; Neon Reef Perch.**
DISTRIBUTION: Indonesian-Australian Archipelago.
HABITAT: Reef areas.
DESCRIPTION: Young fish have a handsome, gleaming, linear pattern on the head and forepart of the body which is broken along the dorsal fin and the stem of the tail. The bands of coloration disappear in old age. Not regularly imported.
LENGTH: To 11 cm ($4\frac{3}{8}$ inches).
CARE: In spite of its aggressiveness, recommended as a single fish when fishes of similar species are not present. It is occasionally sensitive to varying water quality, and will accept all types of animal food.

Emerald Perch; Neon Reef Perch

Blue-green Chromis

FAMILY: Pomacentridae.

SCIENTIFIC NAME: *Chromis caeruleus* (Cuvier and Valenciennes).

POPULAR NAME: **Blue-green Chromis.**

DISTRIBUTION: Shallow coastal regions of the tropical Indo-Pacific region and the Red Sea.

HABITAT: Coral atolls.

DESCRIPTION: This is a lively school fish; coloration graduates from strong blue to greenish to bright green in old age. Frequently imported.

LENGTH: To 13 cm ($5\frac{1}{8}$ inches).

CARE: Should be kept in at least a small school in a coral tank with many hiding places. Take care in acclimatizing; somewhat inclined towards skin infection. Fond of high quality flake food, such as Tetramarin, Tetramin, and Biorel; a plankton eater.

COMMENT: Large schools containing hundreds of these fish are often seen swarming over the coral of the South Pacific. Spawning is said to take place on filamentous algae which has become entangled in the coral. After courtship and spawning, the male guards and cares for the eggs until hatching, which usually takes three or four days.

FAMILY: Pomacentridae.

SCIENTIFIC NAME: *Microspathodon chrysurus* (Cuvier and Valenciennes).

POPULAR NAME: **Atlantic Yellow-tail Damsel Fish; Marine Jewelfish.**

DISTRIBUTION: The tropical Atlantic, Bermuda, southern Florida, and the Caribbean Sea.

HABITAT: Coral reefs.

DESCRIPTION: When young, this is one of the most beautiful pomacentrids of the Caribbean area. As it matures, it turns from blue to black, has sky blue spots all over its body and a milky caudal fin. The adult is brownish with a yellow tail. The fish illustrated is just turning adult.

LENGTH: To 15 cm (6 inches).

CARE: Because it is very aggressive, this fish should be kept only as a single specimen. It even attacks fishes larger than itself. Plant food is recommended.

COMMENT: This is a common species on coral reefs. The young are said to be found frequently among the branches of yellow stinging coral of the genus *Millepora*. This fish feeds in nature on invertebrates, coral polyps, algae and organic detritus.

Atlantic Yellow-tail Damsel Fish

BUTTERFLY FISHES

Butterfly Fishes (family Chaetodontidae) are typical reef dwellers with high, flat, disc-like bodies, enlarged fins, sharply pointed snouts set with bristle-like teeth, and eyes usually camouflaged by dark cross-stripes. Their coloration and patterns are lively. Found in all tropical seas, they are most numerous in the Indo-Pacific region. Their maximum size is about 20 cm (8 inches).

Butterfly Fishes are active daytime swimmers and require plenty of hiding room. Many react aggressively to members of their own species. It is, therefore, easiest to keep single specimens which are not too similar.

Actually, Butterfly Fishes are recommended only for more experienced aquarists. They react sensitively to every worsening of the water and are especially susceptible to flukes or gill-worms. Make sure you buy only medium-sized (5 to 7 cm or 2 to 2¾ inch) fish, as these can most easily be acclimatized to artificial food.

Many Butterfly Fishes are choosy eaters. Acclimatizing them is usually quite difficult, but is easiest with live food (*Mysis, Artemia* or Grindal, a small white worm). Many species may also be fed small *Asellus* species. Plant food is essential.

Threadfin Butterfly Fish

FAMILY: Chaetodontidae.
SCIENTIFIC NAME: *Chaetodon auriga* Forskäl.
POPULAR NAME: **Threadfin Butterfly Fish.**
DISTRIBUTION: Widespread in the tropical reaches of the Indian and Pacific Oceans.
HABITAT: Reef areas.
DESCRIPTION: The head, front and ventral areas, including the ventral fins, are pearl grey tinged with violet. This changes abruptly to deep orange-yellow posteriorly and on the vertical and caudal fins. Behind the black line setting off the head are five greyish-violet lines which run upwards and backwards to the dorsal base. Ten or twelve similar

lines intercept these at right angles. The soft dorsal fin is edged with black, with a large black spot near the margin. The anal fin is yellowish with a black band just inside the edge. The caudal fin is tipped with light violet with two submarginal black bands. In adult fish, the soft part of the dorsal fin at the trailing edge is lengthened out like a streamer. The dark dorsal eye-spot is missing in the adult Red Sea race. Very frequently imported.

LENGTH: To 18 cm ($7\frac{1}{8}$ inches).

CARE: Relatively easy to feed, it will accept flake food, brine shrimp (frozen or newly hatched) and other freeze-dried foods.

FAMILY: Chaetodontidae.

SCIENTIFIC NAME: *Chaetodon chrysurus* (Desjardins).

POPULAR NAME: **Pearlscale Butterfly Fish.**

DISTRIBUTION: Widespread in the Indo-Pacific region, but never plentiful in any given place.

HABITAT: Reef areas.

DESCRIPTION: A large-scaled, very striking species with its pearly scales and red coloration, it is a lively swimmer. Few are imported.

LENGTH: To 15 cm (6 inches).

CARE: Not easy to acclimatize, but once acclimatized, they are not fastidious about food and are relatively hardy.

COMMENT: Like other Butterfly Fishes, this is a rather solitary fish.

Pearlscale Butterfly Fish

Collared Butterfly Fish

FAMILY: Chaetodontidae.

SCIENTIFIC NAME: *Chaetodon collare* Bloch.

POPULAR NAME: **Collared Butterfly Fish.**

DISTRIBUTION: Widespread in tropical reaches of the Indian and Pacific Oceans.

HABITAT: Coral reefs.

DESCRIPTION: This fish is brownish olive with yellow in the middle of each scale. Three bluish-white to white bands cross the anterior: from in front of the dorsal fin, over the operculum and onto the throat; across the preorbital and over the cheek to the throat; over the angle of the mouth and the throat. A similar, fading line marks the forehead. The dorsal and anal fins are tinged with reddish violet. The soft dorsal fin has six bands of black, scarlet and white at its margin. The anal fin is tipped with rows of white, black and scarlet. The caudal fin is red at the base and white posteriorly, divided by a band of black. One of the few dark species, this fish is unmistakable because of the white head stripe on both sides. Quite hardy. Frequently imported.

LENGTH: To 16 cm ($6\frac{1}{2}$ inches).

CARE: Acclimatizes relatively easily. Peaceful. Seems to be rather good-natured among members of its own species. Eats finely chopped food.

FAMILY: Chaetodontidae.
SCIENTIFIC NAME: *Chaetodon ephippium* Cuvier.
POPULAR NAME: **Black-blotched Butterfly Fish; Saddled Butterfly Fish.**
DISTRIBUTION: Particularly the Philippines and Hawaii.
HABITAT: Reef areas.
DESCRIPTION: The body is yellowish brown to yellowish with several greyish bands on the lower sides. A vertical black band runs through the eye and another below the fourth dorsal spine. A quite large black patch edged with a white band running beneath and anteriorly covers most of the rear upper surface of the back. This patch is trimmed posteriorly with orange and white divided by a fine black band. The anal fin is similarly trimmed, although in a more subdued manner. The interior caudal rays have a blackish margin. Seldom imported.
LENGTH: To 20 cm (8 inches).
CARE: Has to be begged to take food. Is peaceful, but also crankier than *Chaetodon auriga*.

Other frequent and recommended species are: *Chaetodon kleini, C. lunula, C. pictus, C. semilarvatus,* and *C. vagabundus*. Somewhat more difficult to keep and less frequently imported are: *Chaetodon capistratus, C. falcula, C. octofasciatus, C. unimaculatus,* and *C. xanthocephalus*.

Black-blotched Butterfly Fish

Be especially warned against the small-nosed forms and species which are known to be choosy eaters: *Chaetodon meyeri, C. trifasciatus,* and *Hemitaurichthys zoster.*

FAMILY: Chaetodontidae.

SCIENTIFIC NAME: *Chelmon rostratus* (Linnaeus).

POPULAR NAME: **Banded Long-snout Butterfly Fish; Beaked Butterfly Fish.**

DISTRIBUTION: Tropical part of the Indian and Pacific Oceans.

HABITAT: Specialized reef dweller of the upper coastal zone.

DESCRIPTION: Jewel of the marine aquarium with its golden bands. Unfortunately very aggressively possessive of living quarters. In nature, they generally live in pairs. The sharp snout can ferret food out of the narrowest crack. Regularly imported.

LENGTH: To slightly over 15 cm (6 inches).

CARE: Hard to acclimatize to food. Easiest to feed live *Mysis, Artemia* and *Tubifex*. Another possibility is the larvae of the gnats of the family Tendipedae (formerly Chironomidae), which are commonly called "bloodworms". Some authorities recommend lowering the density or salinity of the water to a slightly lower hydrometer reading. Provide many hiding places in the aquarium. Keeping single specimens with other species is recommended.

COMMENT: Emaciated fish are probably about to die.

Banded Long-snout Butterfly Fish; Beaked Butterfly Fish

FAMILY: Chaetodontidae.

SCIENTIFIC NAME: *Forcipiger flavissimus* Jordan and McGregor.

POPULAR NAME: **Long-nosed Butterfly Fish.**

DISTRIBUTION: Parts of the Indian and Pacific Oceans, frequently in the region of the Philippines and near Hawaii; sometimes in the offshore islands of Mexico.

HABITAT: Reef areas.

DESCRIPTION: The body is a brilliant yellow which becomes deeper and shaded with orange posteriorly. The upper surface of the head, the nape and side from the tip of the snout to the gill region, is covered with a large triangular dark patch. The lower head and breast are whitish. The caudal fin is greyish while the soft dorsal and anal fins are yellow with a black margin. It is similar to the Beaked Butterfly Fish (*Chelmon rostratus*), but is even more sensitive and more aggressive among members of its own species. The exceedingly long snout indicates that it is a specialist at probing into cracks.

LENGTH: To 20 cm (8 inches).

CARE: Live foods which are of the proper size to be easily ingested are preferable, but fresh chopped table shrimp, frozen brine shrimp, or freeze-dried foods are also acceptable. In spite of initial difficulties, this fish acclimatizes well and can be kept for years.

Long-nosed Butterfly Fish

Poor Man's Moorish Idol

FAMILY: Chaetodontidae.
SCIENTIFIC NAME: *Heniochus acuminatus* (Linnaeus).
POPULAR NAME: **Poor Man's Moorish Idol; Wimple Fish.**
DISTRIBUTION: Widespread throughout the Red Sea, Indian and Pacific Oceans.
HABITAT: Found in small schools in coastal reaches, more frequently in open water.
DESCRIPTION: The body is yellowish white with two broad transverse bands of black. The soft dorsal, caudal and pectoral fins are lemon yellow. The lips are black and there is a black interorbital band above the eyes. Frequently imported.
LENGTH: To 20 cm (8 inches).
CARE: Among Butterfly Fishes, probably the best suited to aquarium keeping. Very hardy and more peaceful than most others. Easy to acclimatize and not particular about food. Not very sensitive in regard to water quality and disease. Best to keep several fish at a time in a tank that is not too small. Grows very quickly. Do not purchase any that are too skinny.

The occasionally imported *Heniochus varius, H. permutatus* and *H. singularis* are somewhat more sensitive.

ANGELFISHES

The Angelfishes (sub-family Pomacanthinae) which, together with the Butterfly Fishes (sub-family Chaetodontinae), compose the family of the Bristle-tooth Fishes (Chaetodontidae), are probably the most magnificent of all sea dwellers. The largest representative can reach a length of 60 cm (24 inches). A main characteristic is the sturdy, backward-directed spine on the under edge of the gill cover.

Angelfishes remain faithful to their local environment and, as reef dwellers, build living quarters for themselves. They are very aggressive towards members of the same species and for this reason should be kept singly or with other Angelfishes that are completely different in both coloration and pattern. Because of their size, pay close attention to the composition of the water. The more places there are in the aquarium to hide, the more they will appear in the open. Adults are frequently found in pairs and are only moderately peaceful. They are peaceful, though, towards other fishes, even very small ones.

The most surprising characteristic of most Angelfish species is the often complete change of coloration and pattern that takes place in the course of growth. This has even led to juvenile and adult forms being described as different species (for example, *Pomacanthus imperator*, juvenile form, has been called *P. nikobariensis*). The often unattractive re-coloration results in a transformation in which even a clear cross-striping can change to lengthwise striping. This transformation usually occurs in fishes from 7 to 10 cm (2¾ to 4 inches), but occasionally in even larger specimens in the aquarium.

Juvenile forms of different Angelfish species can resemble each other. For example, *Pomacanthus asfur, P. annularis, P. imperator, P. maculosus,* and *P. semicirculatus* are all cross-striped with dark blue and white in somewhat similar order. Hence, the juvenile fish are also mutually antagonistic.

In the aquarium, Angelfishes need a great variety of foods; it is most important that you feed them plenty of plant food in the form of algae, lettuce, etc. Angelfishes particularly prefer foods broken into small pieces.

Young fishes are easiest to acclimatize if they are not too small—7 to 10 cm (3 to 4 inches). Large fishes (15 to 20 cm or 6 to 8 inches and larger) cannot usually make the transition satisfactorily; they will refuse to accept artificial food. This is especially true for many species of the genus *Euxiphipops*, and the lovely Royal Empress Angelfish, *Pygoplites diacanthus*. Because Angelfishes are such dainty eaters, never keep them in the same tank with fishes that readily eat their food. In such company the Angelfish is usually the loser, unless you resort to overfeeding, which is just as bad.

Blue King Angelfish (juvenile form)

FAMILY: Chaetodontidae.

SCIENTIFIC NAME: *Pomacanthus annularis* (Bloch).

POPULAR NAME: **Blue King Angelfish; Blue-ringed Angelfish.**

DISTRIBUTION: Tropical Indo-Pacific regions, and the coasts of India and Ceylon.

HABITAT: Widespread reef dweller.

DESCRIPTION: As with many Angelfishes, the adult differs so vastly from the juvenile that they are easily mistaken for separate species. In the juvenile, the ground is black or midnight blue, broken by many blue and white vertical bands, all of which are more or less connected at their outer extremities, near the dorsal and anal bases, by a wavy sky-blue pattern. The dorsal and anal fins are black or midnight blue with a sky-blue outer margin. The caudal fin is without much coloration. The vertical bars on the body are much straighter than on the juvenile form of *P. imperator* (see page 65).

The adult fish shows six or seven gleaming blue diagonal stripes on a golden-brown ground. The pectoral fin is yellow with a blue band at the base. The caudal fin is yellow to whitish with a broad orange tip. There is a blue ring pattern on the shoulder. Regularly imported.

LENGTH: To 40 cm (16 inches).

CARE: Fry can be raised quite easily on suitably diversified food. Well acclimatized fish can be kept for years. This fish is fastidious in regard to water

Blue King Angelfish (adult form)

quality: its tank should be kept free of pollution, uncrowded and well aerated. Frequent partial replacement of the water is also recommended.
COMMENT: As with most Angelfishes, algae or other vegetation is an important dietary component.

Emperor Angelfish (juvenile form)

FAMILY: Chaetodontidae.
SCIENTIFIC NAME: *Pomacanthus imperator* (Bloch).
POPULAR NAME: **Emperor Angelfish.**
DISTRIBUTION: Widespread in warm areas of the Indian and Pacific Oceans; also in the Red Sea.
HABITAT: On reefs far removed from the coast.
DESCRIPTION: The juvenile shows a deep blue-black or black ground with curved, alternating white and blue-white lines (the white lines much broader) which begin almost vertically behind the head,

curving more and more posteriorly until the last form a complete ring just before the caudal fin. The outermost lines form reticulations on the dorsal, anal and caudal fins. The outer dorsal fin is white with a narrow blue margin. The forehead is striped.

The adult is blue-green with up to 20 or more gleaming yellow, narrow, lengthwise stripes. A blue-rimmed, black face mask appears above a pale blue face. The caudal fin is orange-yellow. Regularly imported.

LENGTH: 36 to 40 cm (14 to 16 inches).

CARE: This fish needs a clean, well filtered and aerated tank that is uncrowded and free of pollution due to overfeeding. The pH should be kept high and the ammonia and nitrite levels low. Frequent partial water changes are recommended.

COMMENT: One of the more sensitive species, this fish is especially susceptible to so-called "epidermis sloughing", in which the surface skin, outwards from the side line, disintegrates. The juvenile form has often been described as *"Pomacanthus nikobariensis"*.

Emperor Angelfish (adult form)

Half-moon Angelfish (adult form)

FAMILY: Chaetodontidae.
SCIENTIFIC NAME: *Pomacanthus maculosus* (Forskäl).
POPULAR NAME: **Half-moon Angelfish.**
DISTRIBUTION: The Red Sea.
HABITAT: Reef areas.
DESCRIPTION: Grows large very quickly. Likes to frequent open swimming space. Juvenile form is cross-striped with blue and white, and the cross-stripes vary in width. Very sturdy and long-lived. Not regularly imported.
LENGTH: To 40 cm (16 inches).
COMMENT: Similar to *Pomacanthus asfur*, which grows to only 15 cm (6 inches), but which comes from the same region and is darker blue with a yellow spot on the side and a yellow caudal fin.

French Angelfish (juvenile form)

FAMILY: Chaetodontidae.

SCIENTIFIC NAME: *Pomacanthus paru* (Bloch).

POPULAR NAME: **French Angelfish.**

DISTRIBUTION: Caribbean Sea, tropical Atlantic Ocean.

HABITAT: Reef areas.

DESCRIPTION: Very attractive species, especially in the juvenile form. As the five juvenile yellow cross-stripes vanish, each black scale becomes edged with yellow, forming a subdued coloration network in the adult, every scale having a dark middle. Very hardy; not very aggressive.

LENGTH: To 35 cm (13¾ inches).

COMMENT: The closely related Grey Angelfish, *Pomacanthus arcuatus*, from the same region, grows to 60 cm (23½ inches), but is hardly ever marketed.

FAMILY: Chaetodontidae.
SCIENTIFIC NAME: *Euxiphipops navarchus* (Cuvier and Valenciennes).
POPULAR NAME: **Blue-girdled Angelfish.**
DISTRIBUTION: Sunda Sea, Indonesia; tropical western Pacific.
HABITAT: Reef areas.
DESCRIPTION: This fish has a very large yellow-orange to red-orange saddle area and each scale is dark in the middle. The head and pre-dorsal area is dark; the lower head and throat area from the sub-orbital is yellow to orange. The dark pre-caudal area runs to the anal fin and the belly, and extends to the soft dorsal fin. It is connected with the forward dark pectoral-to-head area. The ventral fin is dark and blue-edged; the pectoral fin is blackish. The caudal fin is yellow-orange to red-orange and both caudal and dorsal fins are blue-edged. The dark and light areas of the body and head are separated by blue streaks. The magnificence of the adult is manifest before full growth is attained. Seldom imported.
LENGTH: Over 20 cm (8 inches).
CARE: Only small fish are easily acclimatized.

Blue-girdled Angelfish

FAMILY: Chaetodontidae.
SCIENTIFIC NAME: *Euxiphipops xanthometopon* (Bleeker).
POPULAR NAME: **Yellow-faced Angelfish.**
DISTRIBUTION: Tropical Indo-Pacific region.
HABITAT: Reef areas.
DESCRIPTION: Scales are blue to violet-black with a bright yellow edge. Around the face, which is violet-black with blue reticulations, is a wide yellow band or "mask" between and including the eyes. The dorsal, caudal and pectoral fins range from clear, bright yellow to orange or even red-orange, the upper edge of the pectoral fin having a blue-black margin. The dorsal fin has a round black spot on the soft portion. Not easy to acclimatize. Imported individually only.

LENGTH: To 25 cm (10 inches).
CARE: Very expensive; do not buy large fish. If you provide many hiding places in the aquarium, the fish appears more often in the open swimming space.

FAMILY: Chaetodontidae.
SCIENTIFIC NAME: *Pygoplites diacanthus* (Boddaert).
POPULAR NAME: **Blue-striped Angelfish; Regal Angelfish; Royal Empress Angelfish.**
DISTRIBUTION: Red Sea and tropical Indo-Pacific region.
HABITAT: Reefs remote from the coast.
DESCRIPTION: In general, this is one of the most

Blue-striped Angelfish

beautiful fish. The upper half of the body is brilliant orange, merging ventrally into lemon yellow. The body is crossed by 8 to 12 wide, curved, pale blue bands with thick brown to black margins. These bands extend onto the dorsal fin. The ventral fin is lemon yellow; the anal fin has curved blue bands edged with darker blue. The head is dark with several blue lines. The lips are yellow. Juveniles have a large black spot on the dorsal fin. Recently somewhat more frequently imported.

LENGTH: To 25 cm (10 inches).

CARE: Up to now, only small fish, up to 10 cm (4 inches), have been acclimatized. Once the transition to the aquarium is complete, these small fish accept a variety of food. When acclimatized as fry, they become very hardy.

FAMILY: Chaetodontidae.

SCIENTIFIC NAME: *Holacanthus ciliaris* (Linnaeus).

POPULAR NAME: **Queen Angelfish.**

DISTRIBUTION: Caribbean Sea, Bermuda, southern Florida, Gulf of Mexico and Bahamas.

HABITAT: Reef areas.

DESCRIPTION: One of the most beautiful species of the Caribbean region, with strong coloration and pattern changes. The young fish have three blue bars on the body and two on the head. The latter border on a dark bar through the eye. The caudal fin is orange-yellow while the dorsal and anal fins are mostly orange with blue margins. Adult fish

have an ocellated forehead spot and long dorsal and anal fins.

LENGTH: To 45 cm (18 inches).

CARE: Very cranky and difficult to care for. Water should be kept at optimum conditions concerning clarity, pH, salinity, and non-pollution. Live or frozen foods of first quality are preferred.

Not quite as handsome, but equally sensitive, is the closely related and variable Blue Angelfish, *Holacanthus isabelita*, which lacks the black, blue-rimmed frontal spot and the trailing blue edges of the dorsal and anal fins.

FAMILY: Chaetodontidae.
SCIENTIFIC NAME: *Holacanthus tricolor* (Bloch).
POPULAR NAME: **Rock Beauty.**
DISTRIBUTION: Caribbean Sea, tropical Atlantic to Bermuda.
HABITAT: Reef areas.
DESCRIPTION: Beautiful fish. Juvenile form yellow with blue-edged, black dorsal spot. The black spreads out later on until it covers most of the body. The head, breast and caudal fin remain bright yellow. The dorsal and anal filaments are prolonged in adults. This fish is an aggressive home builder.
LENGTH: To 60 cm (24 inches).
CARE: Very shy and not easy to care for. Especially susceptible to various skin infections. Extreme variation in food necessary; mix in plant food.

Additional rather hardy species of Angelfish are: *Apolemichthys xanthurus, Chaetodontoplus mesoleucus, Euxiphipops sexstriatus*, and *Pomacanthus semicirculatus*. Both *Holacanthus melanosoma* and *Pomacanthus chrysurus*, however, appear to be difficult to feed and susceptible to disease.

Smaller relatives of the Angelfish comprise the genus *Centropyge*, usually designated as the Pygmy Angelfish. These scarcely reach 10 cm (4 inches), but even so are exceptionally magnificent. (See page 80.)

Rock Beauty

FAMILY: Chaetodontidae.

SCIENTIFIC NAME: *Centropyge argi* Woods and Kanazawa.

POPULAR NAME: **Cherubfish; Pygmy Angelfish.**

DISTRIBUTION: Caribbean Sea, tropical Atlantic Ocean.

HABITAT: Reef areas, usually at depths of 30 m (100 feet) or more, though some specimens have been observed as little as 4.5 m (15 feet) below the surface.

DESCRIPTION: The head and chest are orange-yellow, and around the eye is a narrow blue ring. The body is blue to violet. The dorsal, anal and caudal fins are deep blue with light blue margins. The pectoral fin is pale yellowish. One of the smallest marine species. Very hardy and peaceful. Found regularly among Caribbean imports.

LENGTH: To 6 cm ($2\frac{3}{8}$ inches).

CARE: Should always eat substantially. Food should be as varied as possible and in not-too-large bits. In order to feel secure, this species requires many hiding places in the tank.

Just as hardy, but less frequently marketed is *Centropyge fisheri*, which has a bright, orange-red pattern on the head that runs off to the rear into the steel blue body. More frequently marketed are: *Centropyge bicolor, C. bispinosus, C. kennedy*, and *C. multispinis*. Seldom marketed but very beautiful are: *Centropyge flammeus, C. flavissimus* and *C. potteri* from Hawaii.

Cherubfish; Pygmy Angelfish

WRASSES

Among the approximately 600 species in this extensive family (Labridae) are many magnificent aquarium fish. The extremely slim body is propelled forward through the water solely by the oar-like action of the pectoral fins, with steering accomplished by a backward thrust of the tail. The usually small mouth, provided with protruding and often thick lips, bears powerful teeth which can crack open bottom-dwelling food such as worms, molluscs, crabs and mussels.

Many species bury themselves in loose sand when they sleep or when they are frightened. They certainly require sand in the aquarium to maintain good health. Newcomers to the aquarium especially may vanish for a few days into the sand.

Wrasses are seldom schooling fish, but most construct living quarters. In the spawning season, many species build nests. The male alone takes care of nest building and brood care, and at that time is particularly antagonistic towards members of its own species.

Wrasses are constantly on the move and, for this reason, require a great deal of swimming space. They also need hiding places among coral or in holes, where they like to rest.

They are not particular about their food and will accept a variety of animal food. Their diet should be as varied as possible and certainly should contain some hard-shelled animals such as crabs, small snails and mussels. Plant food is important for all wrasses; otherwise, their growth is affected. With a lack of iodine, they have a tendency towards so-called "lock-jaw".

Always surprising in this family are the often extensive coloration and pattern changes, not only between youth and adulthood, but also between the sexes. Frequent change-overs of sex also occur.

FAMILY: Labridae.
SCIENTIFIC NAME: *Bodianus rufus* (Linnaeus).
POPULAR NAME: **Spanish Hogfish.**
DISTRIBUTION: Caribbean Sea, tropical Atlantic Ocean.

Spanish Hogfish

HABITAT: Common on rocky reefs in 3 to 30 m (10 to 100 feet) of water.
DESCRIPTION: Magnificent coloration in the juvenile stage. Most often red on the upper half of the anterior two thirds of the body, yellow or orange behind and below. Adults are sometimes dark brown with a purplish cast. Grows rather large but only slowly in the aquarium. After acclimatization, this species may be long-lived. In its juvenile period, it serves also as a cleaner fish (see page 94). A lively swimmer. Only occasionally imported.
LENGTH: To 1 m (39¼ inches).
CARE: Requires varied food, otherwise easily satisfied.

FAMILY NAME: Labridae.
SCIENTIFIC NAME: *Coris angulata* Lacépède.
POPULAR NAME: **Clown Labrid; Orange-spot Wrasse.**
DISTRIBUTION: Indian and Pacific Oceans; Red Sea.
HABITAT: Reef areas.
DESCRIPTION: When young (as shown), this fish exhibits very attractive gleaming coloration. It grows quickly, however, and loses its brilliance, becoming mostly darkish or deep green. Large fish are practically monotone in coloration, and have a large forehead lump. Easy to keep, sturdy species. Regularly imported individually.
LENGTH: To 120 cm (about 4 feet).
COMMENT: One of the cleaner Wrasses.

Clown Labrid; Orange-spot Wrasse

(juvenile form)

Clown Wrasse

(adult form)

FAMILY: Labridae.
SCIENTIFIC NAME: *Coris gaimard* (Quoy and Gaimard).
POPULAR NAME: **Clown Wrasse; Gaimard's Rainbowfish; Red Labrid; Red Wrasse.**
DISTRIBUTION: Widespread in the Indo-Pacific region.
HABITAT: Reef areas.
DESCRIPTION: Differences in coloration make the juvenile and adult forms appear to be entirely different species. The young fish is brick red to tomato with 5 black-bordered white areas extending down from the back, plus a black line across the base of the caudal fin. This pattern persists until the fish has reached about 6 cm ($2\frac{1}{2}$ inches) in length.
The adult has small sky-blue dots on a dark background, with a yellow caudal fin and green stripes on the head. Regularly imported.
LENGTH: To 40 cm (16 inches).
CARE: It is best to raise Wrasses from young, as individual fish, or in small groups. A few (2 or 3) fish try to build living quarters and begin fighting among themselves. Carefully acclimatized specimens are easy to keep and are hardy over a long period.
COMMENT: Young fish of the closely related species, *Coris formosa*, are quite similar but can be distinguished: the forehead spot extends down both sides of the head; the first band on the body extends over the entire side; there is an oval dark spot on

the dorsal fin. The adult form of *Coris formosa* is reddish brown with large black spots on the body.

FAMILY: Labridae.
SCIENTIFIC NAME: *Halichoeres centriquadrus* (Lacépède).
POPULAR NAME: **Checkered Wrasse.**
DISTRIBUTION: Reefs of the tropical Indo-Pacific region.
HABITAT: Reef areas.
DESCRIPTION: The body is yellowish brown with broad bluish bands and red streaks on the head. There is a yellow spot below the fourth dorsal spine which is followed by a black blotch. There is also a black spot at the base of the caudal fin. The anal fin has longitudinal bands. In young fish, the dark dorsal spot following the yellow anterior one is black, and, below the last dorsal rays, behind a second light or yellow spot, is another well-developed dark mark. The geometrical body pattern, which is attributed to the scale pattern, develops quite early in the juvenile coloration. Very hardy and undemanding. Occasionally individually imported.
LENGTH: To 30 cm (12 inches).

Checkered Wrasse

FAMILY: Labridae.
SCIENTIFIC NAME: *Pseudocheilinus hexataenia* (Bleeker).
POPULAR NAME: **Six-lined Wrasse.**
DISTRIBUTION: Tropical central and southern Pacific Ocean.
HABITAT: Found among live coral branches and around the bases of large anemones in reef areas.
DESCRIPTION: This is a small fish. The body is a delicate pinkish with bluish undertones. It has six bright red longitudinal lines interspaced with blue, and an ocellus (eye-spot) on the upper part of the base of the caudal fin. A real ornament in a small tank. Only occasionally imported.
LENGTH: To 10 cm (4 inches).
CARE: Quite sensitive and cranky during acclimatization. Food must be extremely varied and tempting, as well as small (live brine shrimp are ideal). Its tank companions should not be too boisterous or aggressive. To maintain good health, requires many small hiding places.

FAMILY: Labridae.
SCIENTIFIC NAME: *Thalassoma bifasciatum* (Bloch).
POPULAR NAME: **Bluehead.**
DISTRIBUTION: Caribbean Sea and tropical Atlantic.
HABITAT: Reef areas.
DESCRIPTION: Striking coloration change occurs; juveniles are greenish yellow with dark flanks and a light belly. The females keep this pattern throughout their lives; the males change. The adult male (shown here) has a blue or green head followed by two wide vertical black bands separated by white or light blue. The rest of the body is green. Adult females occasionally undergo change of sex, in which case their coloration also changes. Young fish serve as cleaner fish (see page 94) and are recognized as such. Less hardy than *Thalassoma lunare* (see next page). Found regularly in Caribbean imports.
LENGTH: To 15 cm (6 inches).
CARE: As a lively swimmer, requires sufficient

room. Demanding in respect to water quality, it must have high pH (preferably 7.8 to 8.2) and saline levels. This fish is sensitive to pollutants, excess ammonia or nitrate in its water. There should be no more than .01 ppm ammonia, or more than 20.0 ppm nitrate. The water should be partially changed (10 per cent) every two weeks. Needs a wide variety of food.
COMMENT: This fish spawns in nature in aggregate or, in the case of large fish, in pairs.

FAMILY: Labridae.
SCIENTIFIC NAME: *Thalassoma lunare* (Linnaeus).
POPULAR NAME: **Lyretail Wrasse; Moon Wrasse; Rainbow Fish.**
DISTRIBUTION: Widespread in the Indo-Pacific region, also in the Red Sea.
HABITAT: Found in areas of abundant coral growth.
DESCRIPTION: One of the most beautiful Wrasses. The fry up to 5 cm (2 inches) in length have a pattern divided lengthwise: the upper side is brown and the underside light blue. The adult fish (shown here) has a violet head with several oblique reddish bands. The body is green, with bands formed by the vertical red streak which occurs on each scale. There is an oblong reddish spot on the pectoral fin. The dorsal fin is red with a blue and yellow margin. The anal fin is violet with a yellow edge, and the caudal fin is green

Lyretail Wrasse

tinted reddish to yellowish. Regularly, if not frequently, imported.

LENGTH: To 30 cm (12 inches).

COMMENT: A recommended species which is quite hardy and not sensitive, this fish hardly ever shows evidence of disease, and, with good feeding, grows continually. Old fish, too, especially the males, remain magnificent. Peaceful; very large specimens are often rough with small fish. Especially lively, they swim a great deal in open water.

Other related and recommended species are: *Thalassoma hardwicke, T. pavo,* and *T. hebraicum; Halichoeres, Lepidaplois, Hemigymnus* and *Anampses* species. The genera *Stethojulis* and *Pseudocheilinus* seem to be more sensitive.

CLEANER FISHES AND THEIR IMITATORS

Only with exceptional difficulty can fish clean themselves, in all parts of the body, of annoying skin parasites, such as crabs. Among the Wrasses—in the wild, at least—there are, however, several species which are specialists at removing the external parasites from other fishes. They maintain regular "cleaning stations", to which they direct other fishes by means of swinging movements. The "customers" come and, in a certain rest position, allow themselves to be treated by the cleaners, who search out the gill space and the mouth openings of even large fish of prey without being eaten. Dead pieces of skin are even carefully removed from wounds or places where the fish have hurt themselves and the wound itself is cleaned out. This is a real symbiotic relationship—both parties have a definite need of each other. The cleaners are also useful in the aquarium.

FAMILY: Labridae.
SCIENTIFIC NAME: *Gomphosus coeruleus* Lacépède.
POPULAR NAME: **Beakfish.**
DISTRIBUTION: Indo-Pacific region.
HABITAT: Coastal waters.
DESCRIPTION: This fish has variable coloration. Sometimes it is not green but violet with yellow vertical fins; dorsal and anal fins have blue edges (the outer edges lighter), and the caudal margins

Beakfish

are either blue or green. The fish illustrated is a male; the female usually sports various tones of brown. Its specialized shape with long, outthrust snout is for penetrating narrow fissures. A very brisk swimmer, it has a spectacular swimming movement. Very hardy.

LENGTH: To 27 cm ($10\frac{3}{4}$ inches).

CARE: After acclimatization, feeding is important. Foods should include live or frozen brine shrimp, chopped fresh shrimp or fish, and green algae. Since it finds every fissure, provide it with plenty of hiding places.

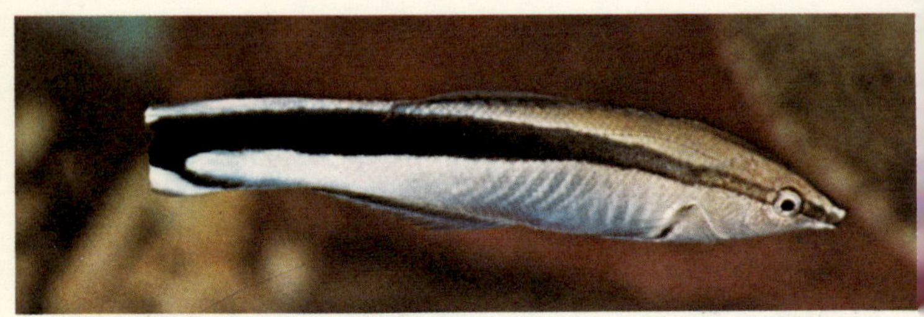

FAMILY: Labridae.
SCIENTIFIC NAME: *Labroides dimidiatus* Bleeker.
POPULAR NAME: **Cleaner Labrid; Cleaner Wrasse.**
DISTRIBUTION: Widespread in the Indo-Pacific region along with several sub-species.
HABITAT: Reef areas.
DESCRIPTION: Very slim species. Fry are blue-black with a blue stripe. Adults are nearly white, the upper anterior surface brownish to tannish. There is a black band which runs from the eye to the upper third of the caudal fin; another black band starts on the anal fin and joins the first on the caudal fin. There is also a dark band on the dorsal fin. Regularly imported in large numbers.
LENGTH: To 10 cm (4 inches).
CARE: Delicate to acclimatize, because you must provide finely chopped food, since the parasites they clean from their tank companions are never enough to keep them fed. You should, however, make it a rule to keep a cleaner fish (if possible, a pair) in every tank.

FAMILY: Labridae.
SCIENTIFIC NAME: *Labroides quadrilineatus* (Rüppell).
POPULAR NAME: **Four-lined Wrasse; Red Sea Cleaner.**
DISTRIBUTION: Red Sea.
HABITAT: Coral reef areas.
DESCRIPTION: The body is brownish or blackish with two longitudinal bright blue bands. The space between the bands is usually darker than the ground or entirely black. The caudal fin has a whitish margin. Less specialized than *Labroides dimidiatus*. Cleaning only seldom observed. Quite hardy. Only occasionally imported.
LENGTH: To 15 cm (6 inches).
CARE: Takes well to substitute or prepared food.

In addition to the genus *Labroides*, there are many other species—many only as fry—which have been observed as cleaners: for example, young Angelfishes and Butterfly Fishes, *Dascyllus* species, the Moorish Idol Fish, and the previously mentioned *Thalassoma bifasciatum* and *Bodianus rufus*.

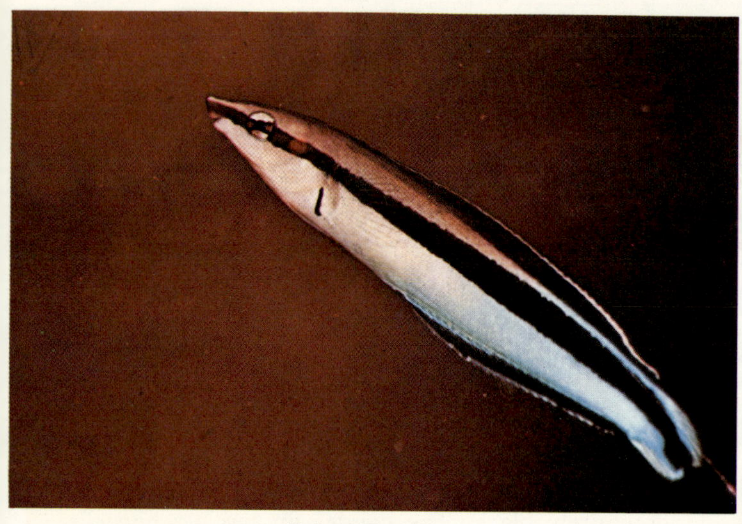

False Cleaner

FAMILY: Blenniidae.

SCIENTIFIC NAME: *Aspidontus taeniatus* Quoy and Gaimard.

POPULAR NAME: **False Cleaner.**

DISTRIBUTION: Same as *Labroides dimidiatus*: the Indo-Pacific region.

HABITAT: Reef areas.

DESCRIPTION: Although the False Cleaner belongs to a different family, it is deceptively like the Wrasses in shape, coloration and even swimming habits. However, it does not clean, but rips off fins

and bits of skin with sharp teeth! Accompanies imports of "cleaner" fish; therefore be careful when buying a cleaner. Principal differentiating characteristics are the underslung mouth and the filament-like ventral fins set very far forward.
LENGTH: To 10 cm (4 inches).

FAMILY: Cirrhitidae.
SCIENTIFIC NAME: *Cirrhitichthys aprinus* (Cuvier).
POPULAR NAME: **Spotted Hawkfish.**
DISTRIBUTION: Tropical Indo-Pacific region.
HABITAT: Reef areas.
DESCRIPTION: Coloration varies with the surroundings. Often not whitish but a pale reddish tan or beige with large red-brown spots. Fine "tufts" of

Spotted Hawkfish

hair-like filaments on the ends of the dorsal fin spines are typical. Hardy. Only occasionally imported.

LENGTH: To 10 cm (4 inches).

CARE: Needs many hiding places. Prefers to lurk on top of high chunks of coral (as shown). This fish is a plankton eater, but it also likes live food.

COMMENT: Like all the members of its family, the Spotted Hawkfish is well adapted to living on coral, to which it can cling with the detached spines of its pectoral fins. It lives mostly in pairs and is aggressive towards members of its own species. Otherwise, it is peaceful. Highly recommended.

Other recommended species are the Caribbean *Amblycirrhites pinos* and the large *Paracirrhites forsteri* and *P. arcuatus*.

FAMILY: Gobiidae.

SCIENTIFIC NAME: *Cryptocentrus cryptocentrus* (Cuvier and Valenciennes).

POPULAR NAME: **Watchman Goby.**

DISTRIBUTION: Indo-Pacific region.

HABITAT: Island (not mainland) coastal waters.

DESCRIPTION: Greyish red with numerous yellowish vertical bars. The anterior portion of the back has blue dots. The head with pale blue dots, has three red, blue-edged streaks on the cheek which are often broken into spots. Gobies are pronounced bottom dwellers that get to know every part of the

Watchman Goby

tank. They are lively, long-lasting fish that receive too little notice and are only occasionally imported.

LENGTH: To 10 cm (4 inches).

CARE: Because they are bottom fish living in holes and hiding places, they are not easy to catch. In the aquarium, therefore, make sure that they actually do eat. These Gobies accept all kinds of food.

COMMENT: The Gobies—which form one of the largest families of fishes (over 400 species)—provide relatively few aquarium fish. Among the Gobies are some very brilliant and striking tropical species whose brood care and symbiotic relationships with crabs are interesting to observe. A family characteristic of Gobies is that both ventral fins have grown into suction discs.

FAMILY: Gobiidae.
SCIENTIFIC NAME: *Gobiosoma* (*Elacatinus*) *oceanops* Jordan.
POPULAR NAME: **Neon Goby.**
DISTRIBUTION: Caribbean Sea and the western Atlantic.
HABITAT: Coral reefs; often found on red coral.
DESCRIPTION: Externally resembles some of the cleaner Wrasses, which it simulates in cleaning ectoparasites from other fishes. An iridescent blue band runs lengthwise between a black midside band and a black mid-dorsal band. Occasionally accompanies Caribbean imports. It is one of the most popular Florida reef fishes.
LENGTH: To 9 cm ($3\frac{1}{2}$ inches).
CARE: Since it is a pronounced bottom fish, make sure that it can reach its food.
COMMENT: Less active in its cleaning habit than some of the Wrasses. Neon Gobies should be bought in compatible pairs if possible; study the fish briefly in the dealer's tank before purchasing. These fish quickly become tame, and have spawned successfully in the aquarium.

Neon Goby

Blue-green Parrot Fish

FAMILY: Scaridae.
SCIENTIFIC NAME: *Callyodon ghobbam* (Forskäl).
POPULAR NAME: **Blue-green Parrot Fish.**
DISTRIBUTION: Red Sea and Indian Ocean.
HABITAT: Coral reefs.
DESCRIPTION: As nearest relatives to the Wrasses, the Parrot Fish have some things in common with them, primarily their way of swimming and the many variations of coloration from young to old and between males and females. In spite of the large size of many species, they are peaceful plant-eaters that browse like cows along the coral banks. Their jaws consist of solid plates made up of teeth grown together, with which they bite off coral branches. They then grind up these chunks with their large gullet teeth. They swallow and digest the coral polyps and other organisms and pass the sand and other refuse out through the anal vent. Only seldom imported.
LENGTH: To 45 cm (18 inches).
COMMENT: Because of these special eating habits, large fish cannot be acclimatized, and in spite of their beauty, they are not fit for the aquarium. Only the skilled aquarist should even attempt to keep fry, but must not be surprised when they lose their decorative coloration.

SURGEON FISHES

The lively and magnificent Surgeon Fishes (Acanthuridae) should certainly be considered as acquisitions for the tanks of the marine aquarist, even though they are usually very aggressive and quite demanding in their care.

Their appearance is permanent although they are capable of quite rapidly changing coloration and pattern at will. They have a high, flat body and on both sides of the tail stalk is an erectible spine which is, as a rule, used as a defensive weapon and can cause painful wounds. The body is covered with the smallest type of scarcely recognizable scales which are, in turn, covered entirely by a slime layer. The typical way Surgeon Fishes swim is to use only the pectoral fins, producing a somewhat peculiar "see-saw flight".

All Surgeon Fishes are plant eaters with rather small mouths, so that an abundant supply of food is necessary, consisting preferably of algae, but also food such as lettuce. Proper diet assures successful keeping of these fishes.

As day-long, lively swimmers, Surgeon Fishes require a great deal of free swimming space, as well as many hiding places, to which they may retreat at night. The less attractive species live companionably in large schools, while, on the other hand, the more magnificent fishes are often severe loners.

All in all, Surgeon Fishes are among the more

difficult fishes to care for, and are best kept singly. You should pay close attention to their compatibility with other fishes, because only a few can be kept in groups. In spite of this, a single Surgeon Fish can not only be the central ornament of a beautiful aquarium, but will also keep the tank free of unwanted algae.

FAMILY: Acanthuridae.

SCIENTIFIC NAME: *Acanthurus coeruleus* Bloch and Schneider.

POPULAR NAME: **Blue Tang.**

DISTRIBUTION: Caribbean Sea and tropical Atlantic Ocean.
HABITAT: Reef areas.
DESCRIPTION: This fish undergoes an especially striking coloration change as it ages. The fry are gleaming yellow and achieve adult bluish coloration when they are about 8 to 10 cm ($3\frac{1}{8}$ to 4 inches) long. This blue increasingly deepens as the soft, dark lengthwise lines broaden. At night, the background brightens and faded, dark cross-stripes become visible. They seem relatively peaceful. The Blue Tang is among the hardier species of Surgeon Fish. Often found in Caribbean imports.
LENGTH: To a maximum of 30 cm (12 inches).
CARE: Should be kept as other Surgeon Fishes.

FAMILY: Acanthuridae.
SCIENTIFIC NAME: *Acanthurus glaucopareius* Cuvier and Valenciennes.
POPULAR NAME: **Philippine Surgeon Fish.**
DISTRIBUTION: Inshore waters of the Indo-Pacific regions to the Philippines, Hawaii, and Mexico.
HABITAT: Turbulent, exposed reef areas.
DESCRIPTION: Black or purplish with bright yellow at the bases of the dorsal and anal fins. The soft part of the dorsal fin has a red area. There is a pearly to white mark beneath and anterior to the eye. The caudal fin is light, darkening posteriorly. This is a relatively sociable species. Very hardy. Imported individually.

Philippine Surgeon Fish

LENGTH: 17 cm ($6\frac{3}{4}$ inches).
CARE: Do not feed too much animal food. Some fishes develop fatty degeneration of the liver when they are fed heavily on a steady diet of animal tissue which has a high fat content in relation to protein. Foods such as white worms or enchytaeids are rather rich and so should be alternated with foods low in fat content, such as chopped, non-oily flounder or halibut, shrimp or crab meat.

Other *Acanthurus* species available on the market are: *Acanthurus chirurgus, A. sohol, A. xanthopterus,* and others. Be warned against the non-hardy *A. triostegus* (silver-white with dark cross-stripes).

FAMILY: Acanthuridae.
SCIENTIFIC NAME: *Acanthurus leucosternon* Bennett.
POPULAR NAME: **Powder Blue Surgeon Fish.**
DISTRIBUTION: Mainly in the Indian Ocean, but also in the Red Sea and the Pacific Ocean.
HABITAT: Reefs and inshore areas.
DESCRIPTION: Very attractive but also aggressive. The body is blue; the dorsal fin yellow; the anal fin whitish at the base and margin, bluish in between. The face is black with a white chin, and there is a light bar behind the head. The caudal fin is whitish to bluish with a bar at the base and another black bar at the extremity; it also has a

whitish or bluish margin. The coloration is unchangeable. Very hardy. Regularly imported.
LENGTH: To 30 cm (12 inches).
CARE: Keep singly only. Middle-sized fish acclimatize best.

FAMILY: Acanthuridae.
SCIENTIFIC NAME: *Acanthurus lineatus* (Linnaeus).
POPULAR NAME: **Clown Surgeon; Striped Surgeon.**
DISTRIBUTION: Indian and Pacific Oceans to the Philippines.
HABITAT: Reefs and inshore waters.
DESCRIPTION: The ground is yellow with a blue or violet belly. Eight or 10 blue lines run horizontally or slightly obliquely from the cheek and eye to the base of the caudal fin. Each of these lines has a brown band on either side as wide as the yellow

Clown Surgeon

ground between. Similar curved bands occur on the cheek. The dorsal and anal fins are dark, and the anterior of the caudal fin has a dark crescent pattern. Not very frequently imported.
LENGTH: To 18 cm (7⅛ inches).
COMMENT: One of the most belligerent, but also the most cheerful-looking, Surgeon Fish. The fry are often very quickly acclimatized, but this species is on the whole less hardy than *Acanthurus leucosternon*.

FAMILY: Acanthuridae.
SCIENTIFIC NAME: *Naso lituratus* (Bloch and Schneider).
POPULAR NAME: **Smoothhead Unicorn Fish.**
DISTRIBUTION: Widespread in the Indian and Pacific Oceans.
HABITAT: Coral reefs.
DESCRIPTION: The body is dusky, the belly faint gold or yellow. Some specimens are olive or brownish. The bands above the eyes are golden or yellow, the lips are red. The dorsal fin is black with a white edge, the anal fin orange, greenish yellow or orange-yellow, and the outer rays of the caudal fin of old fish are filamentous and lengthened. The caudal plates (see below) are surrounded by golden yellow or red. A peaceful, attractive, but not striking fish. Quite hardy. Regularly imported.
LENGTH: To 45 cm (18 inches).

Smoothhead Unicorn Fish

CARE: Abundant plant nutrition is important for all fishes in this genus.

COMMENT: This genus is characterized by the presence of 2, or rarely 3, immovable bony plates on each side of the caudal root which usually bear high, keen-edged, knife-like keels or spines. These spines may be hooked or curved forward and act as formidable weapons. Adults of some species develop a long, slender, conical horn on the forehead before the eyes—thus the popular name.

Caution: All Surgeons should be handled with care, but *Naso* in particular can cut to the bone.

The occasionally imported *Naso brevirostris* and *N. unicornis* are also quite hardy.

Blue Surgeon Fish

FAMILY: Acanthuridae.

SCIENTIFIC NAME: *Paracanthurus hepatus* (formerly *P. theuthis*) (Linnaeus).

POPULAR NAME: **Blue Surgeon Fish.**

DISTRIBUTION: Indian and Pacific Oceans to the Philippines.

HABITAT: Reefs and inshore waters.

DESCRIPTION: The body is a brilliant ultramarine. The base of the pectoral fin is indigo, as is the basal half of the dorsal and anal membranes. There is a broad black band running from the eye to the base of the caudal fin. It connects there with another band that runs below and curves forwards and up, ending under the third dorsal spine. The caudal fin is bright yellow with black margins both above and below. One of the most beautiful species but, unfortunately, the ultramarine fades with increasing age and a washed-out yellow takes its place. Frequently imported; worth the price.

LENGTH: To 25 cm (10 inches).

CARE: Fry are easily acclimatized and can also be kept in groups in suitable sized tanks.

COMMENT: As with other Surgeons and Tangs, this fish requires plant food such as algae or other vegetation.

Moorish Idol

FAMILY: Acanthuridae (sometimes Zanclidae).
SCIENTIFIC NAME: *Zanclus canescens* (Linnaeus).
POPULAR NAME: **Moorish Idol; Kihikihi Loulou; Toby.**
DISTRIBUTION: Probably the only species that is widespread in the Indian and Pacific Oceans.
HABITAT: Coastal reaches up to 50 m (165 feet).
DESCRIPTION: Yellowish white with three broad dark bands. In appearance, resembles the Poor Man's Moorish Idol, *Heniochus acuminatus*. Young specimens have a sharp spine at each corner of the mouth which is lost with age. There were once thought to be two species because of this. Swimming locomotion performed mainly by the board-like pectoral fins (like typical Surgeon Fish). Has very long and thin streamer. Regularly imported.
LENGTH: To 25 cm (10 inches).
CARE: As an eater of plant matter, it is very sensitive to acclimatization and difficult to persuade to eat substitute food. If possible, do not place it in a sterile quarantine tank, but in a tank where algae is growing. Very quarrelsome with members of its own species; death by shock alone is possible. Peaceful towards other fish. Provide lots of swimming room. Large, thickly planted, brightly lit tank is best.
COMMENT: Well acclimatized, singly kept fish are hardy enough to last for years. In spite of its attractiveness, however, recommended only for the experienced aquarist. Only fish in the best condition have a chance of survival.

Sailfin Tang

FAMILY: Acanthuridae.
SCIENTIFIC NAME: *Zebrasoma veliferum* (Bloch).
POPULAR NAME: **Sailfin Tang; Api; Kihikihi; Kihikihi Launui.**
DISTRIBUTION: Red Sea, Indian and Pacific Oceans.
HABITAT: Coral reefs.
DESCRIPTION: Greyish, with 9 or so vertical bands running from the abdomen to the back. Each band has a white edge. Two bands pass vertically through the frontal area, one through the eye. The head is stippled with white or golden spots. The dorsal, anal and caudal fins all have curved blue or white bands; the caudal fin also has light spots. Younger fish tend to be darker to dark brown. When excited, it stretches out its dorsal and anal fins, giving itself an imposing appearance, as well as its most popular name, Sailfin Tang. Regularly imported.
LENGTH: To 40 cm (16 inches).
CARE: Like many of its relatives, the Sailfin Tang is very combative. Thus, it should be kept individually. Since it is also a lively swimmer, it is not suitable for smaller tanks. Take care to buy only young fish (6 to 8 cm or $2\frac{3}{8}$ to $3\frac{1}{8}$ inches) which show no signs of emaciation, since only these can be properly acclimatized. Old fish usually cannot make the transition to the tank. Like Surgeon Fishes, it must also be provided with plant food, upon which it depends. Requires algae if it is not to starve quickly.
COMMENT: Recommended if given attentive care.

Yellow-tailed Tang

FAMILY: Acanthuridae.
SCIENTIFIC NAME: *Zebrasoma xanthurum* (Bleeker).
POPULAR NAME: **Yellow-tailed Tang.**
DISTRIBUTION: Red Sea, Indian Ocean, Ceylon and the east coast of Africa, questionable in the Pacific.
HABITAT: Found around coral reefs.
DESCRIPTION: Can be distinguished from *Zebrasoma veliferum* by its striking snout which is considerably lengthened and comes to a sharp point. The Red Sea variety (shown here) is gleaming blue with a corn yellow tail. In the rest of the distribution region, the background coloration is browner and the tail brighter; the fins are not as strongly broadened. At night, the coloration brightens and there is a dark spot in the middle of the body. Seems to be hardier than *Zebrasoma veliferum*. Is imported, especially from the Red Sea.
LENGTH: To 40 cm (16 inches).
CARE: Recommended for larger tanks. Large fish can be acclimatized.

Similar species that are regularly imported are: *Zebrasoma flavescens* and *Z. scopas*.

RABBIT FISHES

This family (Siganidae), related to the Surgeon Fishes, is characterized by an out-thrust, fixed, munching mouth. The first, shortened spine of the dorsal fin points forward. It is a lively swimmer and a sociable plant eater found in warm coastal waters. The sharp fin rays of many species are poisonous. As aquarium dwellers, Rabbit Fishes require a large tank with a great deal of swimming room. Plant food is necessary for good health. Given a highly varied diet, they are long-lasting fishes that grow well (unfortunately, often too well). Beware of the sharp spines.

FAMILY: Siganidae.
SCIENTIFIC NAME: *Lo vulpinus* (Schlegel and Müller).
POPULAR NAME: **Foxface; Lo.**
DISTRIBUTION: Indonesian-Australian Archipelago and the Pacific Ocean.
HABITAT: Coral areas.
DESCRIPTION: The body and vertical fins are bright yellow. Besides having a throat of dark brown to black, a dark brown or black band runs from this fish's snout through the eye to the front of the dorsal fin. A white band also runs between the dark throat and head regions with a whitish frontal band. A whitish to light yellow area lies behind the pectoral fins. The unmistakable, tube-like, out-

Foxface

thrust mouth is not typical of the family. Has a quiet way of swimming, but is aggressive towards members of its own species. The most attractive species of the family. Only seldom imported.

LENGTH: To 25 cm (10 inches).

CARE: Is quite hardy after acclimatization; can be kept on artificial food, but it also takes animal food.

COMMENT: Use care around this fish, since Rabbit Fishes, including this species, have venomous spines capable of inflicting a painful wound.

Reticulated Rabbit Fish

FAMILY: Siganidae.
SCIENTIFIC NAME: *Siganus vermiculatus* (Cuvier).
POPULAR NAME: **Reticulated Rabbit Fish; Vermiculated Rabbit Fish; Vermiculated Spinefoot.**
DISTRIBUTION: Widespread in the Indo-Pacific region.
HABITAT: Found in inshore waters; occasionally enters brackish and even fresh water.
DESCRIPTION: Body is brown with vermiculated bluish lines everywhere except the belly. The caudal fin is dotted all over with brown. The worm-like, winding, dark pattern of reticulation becomes more intricate with age. Very hardy. Not regularly imported.
LENGTH: To 40 cm (16 inches).
CARE: Relatively easy to acclimatize on animal food. As a lively swimmer, requires considerable open space.

JACK FISHES, SCADS, AND POMPANOS

This fast-swimming family (Carangidae) lives principally in the open sea. The body, which grows large, is usually squeezed flat from the sides; the caudal fin is deeply forked. Only the smallest fry of a few species can be considered for aquarium keeping.

FAMILY: Carangidae.
SCIENTIFIC NAME: *Gnathodon speciosus* (Forskäl).
POPULAR NAME: **Golden Trevally; King Mackerel; Pa'opa'o; Pa'opa'o Ulua; Yellow Ulua.**
DISTRIBUTION: Warm regions of the Indian and Pacific Oceans.
HABITAT: Found in open, offshore water.
DESCRIPTION: The fry are a gleaming, golden yellow, with black cross-stripes. The body then turns dark greenish and the stripes recede sharply. These are lively swimmers in perpetual motion. Only seldom imported.
LENGTH: To 90 cm (36 inches).
CARE: As fry, a delightfully attractive aquarium dweller that prefers the company of large fishes. Unfortunately, they grow very fast. Should only be kept when it is later possible to transfer them to a larger tank. No problems exist in feeding—they accept all kinds of animal food small enough to be easily ingested.

Golden Trevally

FAMILY: Carangidae.
SCIENTIFIC NAME: *Selene vomer* (Linnaeus).
POPULAR NAME: **Horse-head; Look-down; Moonfish.**
DISTRIBUTION: Warm, western Atlantic Ocean from Maine to Uruguay.
HABITAT: Reefs close to the coast.
DESCRIPTION: The body is bluish green above, with silvery sides. Sides are also marked with indistinct vertical bars or dusky blotches. The fins are pale or dusky. The fry have long filaments of skin on the rays of the dorsal and anal fins (as do the Threadfin, genus *Alectis*), which can be many times longer than the body; these vanish later. Hardly ever imported.
LENGTH: To 30 cm (12 inches).
CARE: Unfortunately, it is very sensitive to being transported. Acclimatized fish, however, are very hardy when the necessary swimming space is provided. At first, they must be fed only living food, but later on, all forms of animal food.

Horse-heads; Look-downs

TRIGGERFISHES

Most Triggerfishes (Balistidae) are dwellers in shallow water zones of warm seas. Some are quite magnificent, but are aggressive, not very peaceful loners that attack not only members of their own species but other fishes as well. In spite of this, many Triggerfishes are long-lasting, attractive, easy to keep and suitable for the aquarium. Just be sure that their tank companions are either as large as or larger than they are. In some cases, they should even be kept individually. Sufficient hiding places or retreats are necessary in the aquarium.

Triggerfishes have a high-structured, rhomboid-shaped body, of which the head takes up a third. The mouth is small with a powerful bite; the gill openings are small. They have no ventral fins. The spines of the dorsal fin can be erected and held firmly in place like the "trigger" of a firearm. When danger threatens, the fish squeeze themselves so tightly into a fissure that you have to rip them free if you want to get them out. They swim by means of a waving movement of the soft part of the dorsal and anal fins, often supported by the flat pectoral fins. They often assume unusual "sleeping positions" which can make you think they are dead if you are unfamiliar with this habit.

Some species construct spawning pits and practice brood care; many are poisonous. Many species are demanding in respect to water quality; the oxygen concentration should remain high.

Triggerfishes are not particular about their food and will accept any kind of animal-based food. You must take care, however, to provide hard-shelled animals—crabs, shrimp, edible mussels, and freshwater snails—to give them a chance to use their teeth. Some species also eat echinoderms such as sea urchins and starfish. Others eat sick fish, from which they first tear out the eyes. When searching for food in the sand, they blow a powerful stream of water from their mouths against the bottom.

FAMILY: Balistidae.
SCIENTIFIC NAME: *Balistapus undulatus* (Mungo Park).
POPULAR NAME: **Orange-striped Triggerfish; Undulate Triggerfish; Vermiculated Triggerfish.**
DISTRIBUTION: Indo-Pacific region, widespread distribution as far as the Red Sea.
HABITAT: Coral reef areas.
DESCRIPTION: The body is brownish to olive with numerous undulating yellow to orange-yellow lines from the eye and the back to the anal and caudal fins. The caudal fin is yellow to orange-yellow. Some specimens have a black blotch or black markings at the base of the tail. One of the most aggressive species towards all other fish. Very tough and hardy. Regularly imported as rather large specimens.
LENGTH: To 30 cm (12 inches).
COMMENT: Probably can be kept only with larger, sturdy fish.

Orange-striped Triggerfish

FAMILY: Balistidae.
SCIENTIFIC NAME: *Balistes vetula* Linnaeus.
POPULAR NAME: **Cochino; Old Wench; Old Wife; Peje Puerco; Queen Triggerfish.**
DISTRIBUTION: Tropical parts of the Atlantic Ocean and the Caribbean Sea.
HABITAT: Common on coral reefs, but also found in nearby sand and seagrass areas.
DESCRIPTION: The abdomen and lower head are orange-yellow; the rest of the body is either greenish or bluish grey. There are curved blue bands from the snout to below and before the pectoral fin. Blue, yellow-edged lines mark the head and a blue line circles the lips. The caudal peduncle sports a blue bar. Relatively peaceful except with other *Balistes* species. Grows quickly. Larger fish have long, drawn-out outer rays on the caudal fin. Only occasionally imported.
LENGTH: To 50 cm (20 inches).
CARE: Prefers to eat sea urchins.

Cochino; Queen Triggerfish.

Clown Triggerfish

FAMILY: Balistidae.
SCIENTIFIC NAME: *Balistoides conspicullum* (Bloch and Schneider).
POPULAR NAME: **Clown Triggerfish; Leopard Triggerfish.**
DISTRIBUTION: Widespread in the Indo-Pacific region and the Red Sea.
HABITAT: Reef areas.
DESCRIPTION: One of the most attractive species, but unfortunately quite expensive. Always found alone, but relatively peaceful towards other fish. It exhibits random coloration change, in which the striking black-and-white pattern on the lower half of the body appears to fade. Regularly imported individually.
LENGTH: To 50 cm (20 inches).
CARE: Often difficult to acclimatize; should be fed a wide variety of foods.
COMMENT: The flesh of this fish is poisonous to humans. Ciguatera or "tropical fish poisoning" occurs from time to time in a number of fishes, including food fishes. Toxic fishes which are eaten cause numbness, nausea, paralysis, diarrhoea, spasms, cramps and sometimes even loss of hair. Recovery can take months or even years. Certain fishes, like this species, can be expected to be toxic, while others are only occasionally so.

Pink-tail Triggerfish

FAMILY: Balistidae.

SCIENTIFIC NAME: *Melichthys vidua* Lacépède.

POPULAR NAME: **Pink-tail Triggerfish; Humahuma-hi'u-kole; Humahuma-uli.**

DISTRIBUTION: Tropical parts of the Indian and Pacific Oceans; not uncommon in Hawaii.

HABITAT: Shallow waters of reef areas.

DESCRIPTION: Coloration is usually as shown here, but this fish can also be a glossy black with black-bordered white anal and dorsal fins and a pinker caudal fin. A relatively peaceful and quiet species, but belligerent towards members of its own species. Appears to be susceptible to skin diseases and is rather sensitive.

LENGTH: To 40 cm (16 inches).

Black Triggerfish

FAMILY: Balistidae.
SCIENTIFIC NAME: *Odonus niger* (Rüppell).
POPULAR NAME: **Black Triggerfish; Red-toothed Triggerfish.**
DISTRIBUTION: Widespread in the Indo-Pacific region and the Red Sea.
HABITAT: Reef areas.
DESCRIPTION: Coloration varies. Usually a green or deep blue body, sometimes with an orange-brown undertone. The soft dorsal and anal fins are darker blue, almost violet, with a violet band along the bases. The caudal fin is sky blue. The fry have a gleaming, metallic brass coloration. The forward or anterior rays of the second dorsal and anal fins are longer than those following, and the outer rays of the caudal fin are also extended. A very hardy fish. Regularly imported.
LENGTH: 50 cm (20 inches).
CARE: In the wild this fish eats sponges, but it is easily converted to substitute food.
COMMENT: A very appealing and relatively peaceful species, with several sub-species. Gregarious in the wild. Old fish occasionally jump out of the water: cover the tank!

Picasso Fish

FAMILY: Balistidae.

SCIENTIFIC NAME: *Rhinecanthus aculeatus* Fraser-Brunner.

POPULAR NAME: **Picasso Fish; Humu-humu-nuku-nuku-a-puaa.**

DISTRIBUTION: Indian and Pacific Oceans.

HABITAT: Shallow reef areas.

DESCRIPTION: Looks as if painted by Picasso. Easily recognized by the 3 or 4 rows of black spinelets on the caudal peduncle or base which stand out against the light background. The body is greyish or bluish with a large dark blotch along the side of the body that extends to the anal fin. There are 4 dark inter-ocular bands divided by 3 black bands. Three blue lines run from the eye to the base of the pectoral fin, as does an orange band from the mouth. Four or 5 white bands streak the body from the middle to the anal fin. Regularly imported individually.

LENGTH: To 30 cm (12 inches).

COMMENT: An attractive species with a vibrant, abstract pattern. Becomes more belligerent with age. Similar in character and required care to the Red Sea Picasso Fish, *Rhinecanthus assasi*, and *Rhinecanthus rectangulus*.

FILEFISHES

The Filefishes (Monacanthidae), closely related to the Triggerfishes, have quite flattened bodies and rough skin (hence the name Filefish). Their coloration may change. Instead of ventral fins, Filefishes have an erectile spine, connected to a pocket of skin, which, when erected, enlarges the surface of the body.

Filefishes are quiet swimmers and are relatively shy. They hide easily among plants. Because they eat algae and coral polyps, do not keep them with lower animals. Large species become accustomed to artificial food relatively easily.

FAMILY: Monacanthidae.
SCIENTIFIC NAME: *Amanses sandwichiensis* (Quoy and Gaimard).
POPULAR NAME: **Sandwich Filefish; Sandwich Trigger.**
DISTRIBUTION: Widespread in practically all tropical seas.
HABITAT: Often found drifting in Sargassum weed, which its variable coloration effectively matches.
DESCRIPTION: Quite variable coloration: sometimes plain brown to blackish; sometimes brown spotted body divided by white lines. Other specimens may be brownish with darker spots or entirely purplish black with orange dorsal and anal fins. Only occasionally imported.

Sandwich Filefish

LENGTH: To 38 cm (15 inches).
CARE: This fish has a small mouth. Therefore, feed it food that is not too large. It is especially fond of polyps, such as *Glasrosen*.
COMMENT: Capable of instant coloration changes and camouflages; the random markings can change with mood (for example, the network pattern can vanish in seconds).

FAMILY: Monacanthidae.

SCIENTIFIC NAME: *Oxymonacanthus longirostris* (Bloch and Schneider).

POPULAR NAME: **Long-nosed Filefish; Orange Filefish.**

DISTRIBUTION: Indian and Pacific Oceans.

HABITAT: Found in shallow reef waters, especially among staghorn coral.

DESCRIPTION: An oblong body, with a snout much longer than in other monacanthids. Usually blue, sometimes with a slight greenish cast, it is darkest on the upper part of the head and very pale towards the caudal base. It sports 6 or 7 rows of orange spots on the body as well as orange stripes on the head. These stripes converge at the snout, which is tipped with white. The dorsal spine is orange. Imported fairly regularly.

LENGTH: 10 cm (4 inches).

CARE: Single specimens are very weak and should be kept in small groups. Transition of these polyp eaters to the aquarium is not easy. Feed them small crabs and *Artemia*, but also various dried foods. Later, feed such foods as finely chopped mussels and crab meat. Keep with quiet and smaller fish; otherwise, they will not accept food. Be sure the tank has plenty of algae.

COMMENT: A vibrant, extraordinarily attractive species that remains small but which is, unfortunately, not simple to care for.

Long-nosed Filefish

TRUNKFISHES, BOXFISHES, AND COWFISHES

The "box" or "trunk" for which these fishes (Ostraciontidae) are named is constructed of flat, interconnected ossifications which form a second skeleton, into which the fish, with its normal skeleton, is inserted. The fish retains its ability to move through openings in the outer skeleton for fins, eyes, mouth and gills. It swims only with the dorsal and anal fins, supported by the pectoral fins; it has no ventral fins. The tail, capable of steering, helps the fish turn on the spot. The body shape may be triangular, quadrangular or pentagonal in cross-section. Trunkfishes, found in all warm seas, are lively fish in spite of their rigid construction. They are very manageable and appealing aquarium dwellers, although, unfortunately, they do present problems in keeping. Watch for starved fish with sunken flanks and for specimens that are too big, as these will not survive acclimatization. Thin Trunkfishes, whose ossification-covered bodies are delicate, have a tendency towards skin irritations.

Trunkfishes can secrete a dangerous poison when netted or otherwise distressed, which is still lethal when they are dead, and can kill the entire population of a tank. Although they are aggressive among themselves, they are peaceful towards other fishes.

Small-mouthed Trunkfishes eat plankton. Live food and other plant foods also appear to be important.

Well acclimatized specimens are quite hardy.

FAMILY: Ostraciontidae.
SCIENTIFIC NAME: *Lactoria cornuta* (Linnaeus).
POPULAR NAME: **Long-horned Cowfish.**
DISTRIBUTION: Indian and Pacific Oceans. Often carried long distances by ocean currents.
HABITAT: Shallow waters near bottom.

Long-horned Cowfish

DESCRIPTION: Easily recognized by its long horns, which have pronounced ridges in young fish. In older specimens, the horns are nearly smooth. The body is a pale greenish yellow with dark bands. Except for the belly, which is a clear yellow, there is a bluish or whitish pearly spot on the scales. The lips are yellowish with a broad, blackish line behind them. As the fish grows, the caudal fin becomes disproportionately large. This fish stays continuously in motion in open water. Not imported regularly.
LENGTH: To 50 cm (20 inches).
COMMENT: This species is relatively easy to acclimatize as fry. Wounds in the skin, especially damage to the horns, often heal poorly or not at all.

FAMILY: Ostraciontidae.
SCIENTIFIC NAME: *Ostracion tuberculatus* (Linnaeus).
POPULAR NAME: **Black-dotted Trunkfish; Boxfish.**
DISTRIBUTION: Indian and Pacific Oceans.
HABITAT: Reef areas.
DESCRIPTION: The fry are yellowish with black dots. A pattern change and body lengthening becomes evident in the course of growth. Older fish turn darker and their spots can be bluish white in the middle. The body is short, thick-set and cube-shaped. Quite hardy and peaceful. Fry occasionally imported.
LENGTH: To 45 cm (18 inches).

Black-dotted Trunkfish

FAMILY: Ostraciontidae.
SCIENTIFIC NAME: *Tetrasomus gibbosus* (Linnaeus).
POPULAR NAME: **Camel Trunkfish; Pyramid Trunkfish.**
DISTRIBUTION: Warm reaches of the Indo-Pacific region.
HABITAT: Usually found in shallow waters near the bottom.
DESCRIPTION: This fish has a roughly triangular body, with small spines pointing upward over each eye and 4 additional spines on the ventrolateral ridges pointing backward. It is brownish yellow with a paler yellow on the underside. There are several dark or dusky spots or bars on the lower sides and a similar spot on the dorsal spine. The base of each vertical fin is marked with an obscure dark spot. Regularly imported individually.
LENGTH: To 30 cm (12 inches).
COMMENT: One of the most bizarre-looking species. It is a very hardy fish, but somewhat inclined towards skin diseases.

Camel Trunkfish

PORCUPINE FISHES

Closely related to the Puffers, Blowfishes and Globefishes (see page 158), the Porcupine Fishes (Diodontidae) have permanently erect or erectile spines in the outer skin (epidermis) which stand out rigidly from the body when the foregut is blown up with water or air. In addition, all the teeth in the upper and lower jaws are fused into a tooth-plate (hence the name *Diodon* meaning two-tooth). This powerful set of teeth effortlessly cracks mussels, snails and crabs, which compose the principal food of these fishes. Porcupine Fishes swim, for the most part, by moving their big, fan-shaped pectoral fins.

About 15 species of Porcupine Fishes are known to frequent the coastal regions of all warm seas. All can be kept very well in the aquarium if they are provided with plenty of oxygen, for which they have an exceptional need. Take care in acclimatization that the fish do not blow themselves up with air, as it is often very hard for them to return to normal size. They should also have sufficient opportunity to exercise their teeth; include whole mussels, fresh-water snails and crabs in their diet. These foods are also good for their intestines.

In a small tank, Porcupine Fishes tend to fight among themselves, but are peaceful towards other fishes. While eating or grasping with their strong teeth, however, an occasional "error" can be made, and they may bite other fishes. In a community tank, Porcupine Fishes are good indicators for the presence of *Cryptokarion* or *Oodinium* infections, to which they are very susceptible.

FAMILY: Diodontidae.
SCIENTIFIC NAME: *Chilomycterus schoepfi* Walbaum.
POPULAR NAME: **Burrfish; Spiny Boxfish.**
DISTRIBUTION: The Caribbean and Atlantic coasts of the United States.
HABITAT: Shallow waters.

Spiny Boxfish

Porcupine Fish

DESCRIPTION: Yellowish green to brownish with dark linear markings. There is an ocellated spot beneath the dorsal fin, and others behind the pectoals. Even when the fish is in a position of rest, the spines jut out, giving the fish a very bizarre appearance. The fry, especially, have a long, weak tentacle over each eye. Rather a good-natured species. Quite hardy; becomes tame after acclimatization.
LENGTH: To 25 cm (10 inches).

FAMILY: Diodontidae.
SCIENTIFIC NAME: *Diodon holacanthus* Linnaeus.
POPULAR NAME: **Porcupine Fish; Spiny Puffer.**
DISTRIBUTION: All tropical seas.
HABITAT: Reef areas.
DESCRIPTION: Brownish grey above, nearly white beneath, with a series of broad, velvety brown transverse bands and spots. The first runs from eye to eye and downward to a pointed stripe on the underside; the second runs midway between the first and the pectoral fin; a third, crescent-shaped spot lies behind the pectoral fin. Other spots occur on the middle of the back and at the base of the dorsal fin. Quite hardy. Only occasionally imported.
LENGTH: To 50 cm (20 inches).
CARE: Peaceful, but at first shy among other fishes. Keep it, therefore, only with other quiet specimens.

PUFFERS, GLOBEFISHES OR BLOWFISHES

What was said about the Porcupine Fishes (see page 154) is also true for Puffers (Tetraodontidae). The teeth are fused on both sides of the jaw (*Tetraodon* means four-tooth). The round body can be blown up. The skin is tough and without scales. Many Puffers are poisonous.

This family is rich in species found in all warm seas—some species are even found in brackish and fresh water. As aquarium fish, Puffers are easy to keep and quite hardy if you care for them as you do for the Porcupine Fishes (see page 154). They do, however, tend to fight among themselves. Also, while propagating, the male bites into the female and holds on fast.

Puffers eat almost anything you give them. They have a tendency to seize any tank decoration that is not too compact, such as fan coral and stone coral.

FAMILY: Tetraodontidae.

SCIENTIFIC NAME: *Amblyrhynchotus diademata* (Rüppell).

POPULAR NAME: **Masked Globefish; Masked Puffer.**

DISTRIBUTION: Red Sea.

HABITAT: Reef areas.

DESCRIPTION: The entire body is nearly uniformly greenish or whitish. The mouth is black to brown and a broad black or brown band runs through the

Masked Globefish

eyes and on to the gill openings. The fins are dark. Quite hardy. Mostly imported as large, single specimens.

LENGTH: To 30 cm (12 inches).

CARE: Should not be put into the same tank with members of its own species and other Puffers.

FAMILY: Tetraodontidae.
SCIENTIFIC NAME: *Arothron nigropunctatus* (Bloch and Schneider).
POPULAR NAME: **Lemon Globefish; Citron Puffer.**
DISTRIBUTION: Indian Ocean, as far as the Red Sea.
HABITAT: Reef areas.
DESCRIPTION: The entire body is a beautiful lemon yellow. There are scattered spots on the side, irregular small and large black spots on the back, one large blotch around the base of the dorsal fin, and large round spots around the eye and gill openings. These dark spots vary in prominence. Some specimens are simply yellow with a few black dots. Juvenile form is a nondescript olive. Seldom imported.
LENGTH: To 50 cm (20 inches).

Other Puffers regularly imported are: *Arothron stellatus, A. aerostaticus, A. hispidus, A. reticularis,* and *Sphaeroides spengleri.*

Lemon Globefish

FAMILY: Tetraodontidae (formerly Canthigasteridae).
SCIENTIFIC NAME: *Canthigaster papua* (Bleeker).
POPULAR NAME: **Peacock-eyed Sharp-nosed Puffer.**
DISTRIBUTION: Tropical and sub-tropical Indian and Pacific Oceans.
HABITAT: Around reefs and inshore waters.
DESCRIPTION: Brown body, paling on the belly, and covered with markings that, on the upper side, run together to form transverse or angular bluish, dark-edged lines. The snout, sides and caudal fin are spotted with yellowish, dark-edged ocelli the size of the pupil of the eye. Characteristic is the large blue-edged ocellus under the dorsal fin. Regularly imported.
LENGTH: To no more than 15 cm (6 inches).

Other related species are: *Canthigaster benetti, C. janthinopterus* and *C. valentini.*

Peacock-eyed Sharp-nosed Puffer

Fairy Basslet; Royal Gramma

FAMILY: Grammidae.
SCIENTIFIC NAME: *Gramma loreto* Poey.
POPULAR NAME: **Fairy Basslet; Royal Gramma.**
DISTRIBUTION: Caribbean Sea.
HABITAT: Dwells in caves, beneath ledges, at depths up to 60 m (200 feet).
DESCRIPTION: The front of the body is purple or violet, the back bright yellow or orange. A black spot is found on the anterior of the dorsal fin. The fry are occasional cleaners. A splendid, hardy, small species. Found regularly in Caribbean imports.
LENGTH: To 6 cm ($2\frac{3}{8}$ inches).
CARE: Not particular about food. You should, however, guard against the possibility of food rivalry by not keeping it in the same tank with small, quiet fish.
COMMENT: The adult is a loner who is not always visible (he turns his belly towards walls and the ceiling). A good jumper. Fry have been hatched out in the aquarium but have not yet been successfully raised. Nest building with algae and small bits of staghorn coral is often observed.

Lyretail Coralfish

FAMILY: Serranidae (formerly Anthiidae).
SCIENTIFIC NAME: *Anthias squamipinnis* (Peters).
POPULAR NAME: **Lyretail Coralfish.**
DISTRIBUTION: Indian and Pacific Oceans.
HABITAT: Lives in large swarms on the outer (seaward) side of reefs as well as in fissures on rocky coasts.
DESCRIPTION: Coloration varies: yellow to bright orange-yellow, sometimes pink. The male has lengthened fins. Peaceful towards its tank companions. Not regularly imported.
LENGTH: 10 to 12 cm (4 to $4\frac{3}{4}$ inches).
CARE: Should be kept in groups in the aquarium; single specimens are very weak. A plankton eater, it nevertheless requires a wide variety of other small foods, such as small crabs. A tank with many hiding places and adequate swimming space is also necessary.
COMMENT: A lovely species that remains small. Several relatives with similar coloration are imported less frequently.

CARDINAL FISHES

Cardinal Fishes (Apogonidae) are found almost exclusively in tropical seas, but a few species inhabit brackish and fresh water. In the aquarium, many species are very demanding in respect to water purity, pH, salinity and ammonia levels. Their bodies are usually flattened or spindle-shaped and remain small. They have two separate, narrow dorsal fins, located directly opposite the ventral and anal fins, and big eyes.

On the whole, Cardinal Fishes are pleasing and generally visible in daylight in open water when they are looking for plankton. The coloration of the species may vary. The reddish species especially are twilight and cave fishes.

Not all species are equally hardy. Many are mouth breeders with previous, internal fertilization. Although brood care, attended to by the male, is often observed in the aquarium, the fry are very small and up to now (1974) have not been raised to maturity in the aquarium.

Most Cardinal Fishes are not demanding in regard to food and will feed well if no small, agile competitors are present.

Flamefish

FAMILY: Apogonidae.
SCIENTIFIC NAME: *Apogon maculatus* (Poey).
POPULAR NAME: **Flamefish.**
DISTRIBUTION: Western Atlantic and Caribbean.
HABITAT: Shallow waters.
DESCRIPTION: Bright red with a round black spot beneath the second dorsal fin and another broad dark spot on the caudal peduncle. There is a longitudinal dusky band on the head and a dusky spot on the operculum or gill cover. A large-eyed twilight fish, it often hides and watches for food competitors. Very quiet. Acclimatized specimens are very hardy.
LENGTH: 10 to 15 cm (4 to 6 inches).
COMMENT: This is probably the most common Cardinal Fish in the West Indies.

FAMILY: Apogonidae.
SCIENTIFIC NAME: *Apogon nematopterus* (Bleeker).
POPULAR NAME: **Pajama Cardinal Fish; Pennant Cardinal Fish.**
DISTRIBUTION: Indian Ocean, as far as the western Pacific.
HABITAT: Inshore waters.
DESCRIPTION: Olive brown, with a dark or black band from the first dorsal fin to behind the ventrals. The head is often spotted with black and the posterior half of the body spotted with red-brown. Quite hardy. Regularly imported.
LENGTH: To 8 cm ($3\frac{1}{8}$ inches).
COMMENT: Appealing species. Long, drawn-out pennant streamers on the dorsal fins are a sign of a well-kept adult fish. Can be seen standing motionless in open water. Spawning is often observed.

Pajama Cardinal Fish

BATFISHES

Characteristic of all the species of this family (Ephippidae) are the elongated, sail-like dorsal and anal fins set on the disc-like body. The hard and soft parts of each fin combine to create a solid surface. The fry, whose fins are especially lengthened, often spin about just under the water's surface, like so many leaves in a wind.

Found along tropical coasts, and in mangrove and brackish water stretches, Batfishes are sturdy, omnivorous creatures, that do not even shy away from eating waste material. They are very hardy in the aquarium, but, unfortunately, they grow much too fast, having an annual rate of growth that can be as high as 30 cm (12 inches) per year. They require a great deal of room, vertically as well as horizontally.

Batfishes are aggressive when kept as a small group; when more than four of the same size are kept, however, they get along well together. Injuries regenerate quickly. A large group eats all animal food, thus ensuring good water quality.

Batfishes are very easily frightened and irritated by lively little fish. They do not allow themselves to be cleaned by *Labroides*.

Orbiculate Batfish

FAMILY: Ephippidae.
SCIENTIFIC NAME: *Platax orbicularis* (Forskäl).
POPULAR NAME: **Orbiculate Batfish; Round Batfish.**

Orange-ringed Batfish

DISTRIBUTION: Indian Ocean and the western Pacific; also the Red Sea.
HABITAT: Coastal waters.
DESCRIPTION: Dusky to orange-brownish with a black ocular band which is more or less distinct. The fins have black edges; the last two-thirds of the ventral fins are yellow. The fry have small fins and often their bodies are covered with white dots. The closed mouth area always forms a somewhat out-thrust angle. The adult is very similar to *Platax teira*. This is the most frequently imported of the Batfishes.
LENGTH: To 60 cm (24 inches).
COMMENT: When buying, beware of emaciated specimens; these are often heavily infested with parasites.

FAMILY: Ephippidae.
SCIENTIFIC NAME: *Platax pinnatus* (Linnaeus).
POPULAR NAME: **Long-finned Batfish; Orange-ringed Batfish.**
DISTRIBUTION: Indonesian-Australian Archipelago.
HABITAT: Coastal waters.
DESCRIPTION: By far the most striking Batfish species. Attractive dark brown body with silver-grey stripes, framed, including the ventral fins, with an orange-red stripe which fades with age.
LENGTH: 30 cm (12 inches).
CARE: More difficult to acclimatize and crankier than other Batfish species.

Long-finned
Batfish

FAMILY: Ephippidae.

SCIENTIFIC NAME: *Platax teira* (Forskäl).

POPULAR NAME: **Long-finned Batfish.**

DISTRIBUTION: Indian Ocean and the western Pacific.

HABITAT: Coastal waters.

DESCRIPTION: The fry have greatly lengthened fins, which can extend for several body widths. As the fish gets older, the fins shorten and the body pattern (shown in photograph) practically disappears. These fish have an evenly rounded off mouth region, characteristic of the species. Seldom imported.

LENGTH: To 60 cm (24 inches).

CARE: Often sensitive in acclimatization, frequently injuring the fins. If this happens, the best thing to do is cut the fins off straight; otherwise they will grow crooked and be unsightly.

FAMILY: Ephippidae.

SCIENTIFIC NAME: *Drepane punctata* (Linnaeus).

POPULAR NAME: **Spotted Drepane; Spotted Sickle Fish; Spotted Spade Fish.**

DISTRIBUTION: Tropical Indo-Pacific region, as well as the tropical West African coast.

HABITAT: Found in coastal reaches and on river deltas.

DESCRIPTION: Silvery, with about 10 vertical rows of dots over the back and downward past the midside. The ventral fins are dusky at the tips. Strong spines exist in the hard part of the dorsal and anal fins; the pectoral fins are sickle-shaped. The mouth can be extended like a snout. A sturdy species that greatly resembles other Batfishes. Seldom imported.

LENGTH: To over 30 cm (12 inches).

CARE: Requires extensive swimming room and a wide variety of food, including plant material.

Spotted Drepane

Fingerfish; Mono

FAMILY: Monodactylidae.

SCIENTIFIC NAME: *Monodactylus argenteus* (Linnaeus).

POPULAR NAME: **Fingerfish; Mono; Silver Leaf Fin.**

DISTRIBUTION: Shallow coasts of the Indian and Pacific Oceans.

HABITAT: Found in stretches of mangrove and river outlets in brackish water; the young fish can even endure fresh water. Mature in the shallow coastal zones.

DESCRIPTION: Silvery with yellowish undertones which become less intense with age and size. There is a black orbital band and another band at the posterior margin of the operculum. The caudal and pectoral fins are yellow, the dorsal and anal fins greyish. Quite frequently imported.

LENGTH: To 20 cm (8 inches).

CARE: Recommended for beginners, but always keep a group of 4 or 5 specimens and allow plenty of swimming space. When buying, choose lively and bright specimens; dark coloration is a sign of fear and also a symptom of illness.

COMMENT: This is a very lively school fish that will eat small fishes, but also eats plant food, which should be provided for it in the aquarium.

Spotted Scat

FAMILY: Scatophagidae.
SCIENTIFIC NAME: *Scatophagus argus* (Gmelin).
POPULAR NAME: **Spotted Scat.**
DISTRIBUTION: Indian and Pacific Oceans.
HABITAT: Inhabits the mouths of rivers and mangrove coasts, especially as fry. Later found in shallow coastal reaches.
DESCRIPTION: Yellowish white with a bluish wash. The body is covered with numerous round blue or black spots; these are proportionately larger in young fish. Very frequently imported.
LENGTH: To 30 cm (12 inches); in the aquarium, usually under 20 cm (8 inches).
CARE: Plant food is very important for aquarium-kept fish. These should be kept in small groups of at least 4 or more; otherwise they become quite unsociable. The fry may be kept in brackish water, but later they feel better in salt water. Do not make the transition too quickly. When buying, watch for clean fins: this fish is often susceptible to *Lymphocystis*. Very sturdy.
COMMENT: Quite suitable for the beginner to keep. Omnivorous; also eats excrement (hence the name *Scatophagus*).

The juvenile form of the red-patterned "subspecies", *Scatophagus argus rubrifrons,* is also quite easy to care for.

FAMILY: Theraponidae.
SCIENTIFIC NAME: *Therapon jarbua* (Forskäl).
POPULAR NAME: **Jarbua; Stripey; Target Fish.**
DISTRIBUTION: Widespread in the Indo-Pacific region.
HABITAT: Found in coastal areas and river mouths.
DESCRIPTION: The body is a light silvery grey with a light yellowish green on the top half; the sides sometimes have a light violet cast. There are several lengthwise black bands on the upper sides which are prominent in young fish, but fade with age and growth. The tip of the dorsal fin is black; the caudal fin is dark-tipped and more or less banded. Young fish build small shelters for themselves in holes they dig in the sand; they are very aggressive, as well as easily frightened. They have sharp spines on the gill covers. Not until adulthood are they somewhat more peaceful as they congregate in groups; however, they then require a great deal of swimming room. Frequently imported as a fresh-water fish.
LENGTH: To 30 cm (12 inches).
CARE: Not demanding in regard to food; eats anything of an animal nature.
COMMENT: A sturdy fish of prey which can grow quite large and can live part of its life in brackish water. Because of its rapid growth and aggressiveness, not recommended.

Jarbua; Stripey; Target Fish

FAMILY: Toxotidae.

SCIENTIFIC NAME: *Toxotes microlepsis* (Günther).

POPULAR NAME: **Archer Fish.**

DISTRIBUTION: Coasts of the Indian and Pacific Oceans, especially in the Sunda Sea of Indonesia.

HABITAT: Often found in river bank regions; they enter deeply into the mouths of rivers. For a long time, they have also been kept in fresh water. Adult fish, however, require brackish water in which to spawn.

DESCRIPTION: Yellow-green to brownish above, with greenish-grey sides and a silvery white underside. Black blotches or bands of variable shape and position mark the head and body. A pronounced surface fish. Quite frequently imported.

LENGTH: To 20 cm (8 inches).

CARE: Easily kept: fill tanks only half way and furnish with river bank growth. Keep fish either singly in a small tank or in great numbers in a large tank with plenty of space. If too crowded, they become unsociable. The surface of the water should not be disturbed. They will eat living insects and other animal food.

COMMENT: This fish "shoots" for its food when live bait is offered in exposed places. The bait must be far enough away from the surface to make shooting for it necessary. Recommended for the beginner to keep.

Archer Fish

SWEETLIPS

Most of the members of this very attractive, Indonesian-Australian group (family Pomadasyidae), related to the Perches and Grunts, have puffy lips and large heads. The coloration is lively, especially in the juvenile stages, but there is a noticeable change in coloration and pattern, which hinders systematic classification. The large pectoral fins make typical waving movements, a characteristic that is later lost.

Sweetlips are omnivorous, but they are not especially hardy in the aquarium. For good health, the fry, at least, should be given a wide variety of living food; for the cautious eater, try withholding food for a time to build up its appetite. Plant food also seems beneficial.

Younger Sweetlips live in groups, and some adult species are schooling fish. They are lively swimmers, so provide sufficient swimming room. They are very peaceful towards smaller tank companions.

FAMILY: Pomadasyidae (formerly Plectorhynchidae).

SCIENTIFIC NAME: *Plectorhynchus albovittatus* (Rüppell).

POPULAR NAME: **Yellow-lined Sweetlips.**

DISTRIBUTION: Central Indo-Pacific region.

HABITAT: Coral reefs.

DESCRIPTION: Very attractive juvenile coloration with gleaming, orange-yellow stripes; however, it

Yellow-lined Sweetlips

grows fast and its adult coloration is more or less dirty brown with black fin spots. Very hardy. Regularly imported at intervals.

LENGTH: To 60 cm (24 inches).

CARE: This is the best Sweetlips species to acclimatize. Food should be varied; it especially likes live crabs.

COMMENT: While the popular and more descriptive name is "Yellow-lined Sweetlips", the scientific name *albovittatus* means "white-lined". This probably arose from studying specimens stored in alcohol, in which the lines would appear white.

Clown Sweetlips

FAMILY: Pomadasyidae (formerly Plectorhynchidae).
SCIENTIFIC NAME: *Plectorhynchus chaetodonoides* (Lacépède).
POPULAR NAME: **Clown Sweetlips.**
DISTRIBUTION: The Indonesian-Malaysian Archipelago and western Pacific.
HABITAT: Coral reefs.
DESCRIPTION: Very unusual-looking, with especially large fins. The young fish look as if they were white fish wearing a brown pull-over with big holes in it. The brown areas later turn into spots, and in adults, form a recognizable network; in older fish, the brown is distributed over the entire body. Occasionally inclined towards attack from flukes. Fairly regularly imported.
LENGTH: To 45 cm (18 inches).
CARE: Unfortunately, a quite sensitive species. Not until they have been acclimatized and begin to grow can you depend on being able to keep them alive for any length of time. Should be fed a wide variety of food.

FAMILY: Pomadasyidae (formerly Plectorhynchidae).
SCIENTIFIC NAME: *Plectorhynchus orientalis* (Bloch).
POPULAR NAME: **Oriental Sweetlips.**
DISTRIBUTION: Central Indo-Pacific region and the Red Sea.
HABITAT: Coral reefs.
DESCRIPTION: Very attractive. Juvenile has large yellowish or cream spots on a dark chestnut ground. With age, these spots change little by little into lengthwise stripes. Still quite vibrant in adulthood. More or less regularly imported.
LENGTH: To 40 cm (16 inches).
CARE: Very delicate. Needs careful watching and feeding in acclimatization. Keep with quiet fish. Many specimens grow thin even if well fed; for this reason, buy well nourished specimens.
COMMENT: Occasionally, gold forms appear.

FAMILY: Pomadasyidae (formerly Plectorhynchidae).

SCIENTIFIC NAME: *Spilotichthys pictus* (Thunberg).

POPULAR NAME: **Painted Sweetlips.**

DISTRIBUTION: Tropical Indo-Pacific region.

HABITAT: Coral reefs.

DESCRIPTION: The fry have striking black and white or chestnut and white lengthwise stripes which turn gradually into spots. Adults are silver-grey with a dark pattern of dots on the upper half of the body. The middle of the back is dark. Very hardy. Only occasionally imported.

LENGTH: To 50 cm (20 inches).

CARE: A slow eater, but relatively easy to acclimatize.

GRUNTS

Closely related to the Sweetlips and Snappers, Grunts (Pomadasyidae) produce tones by grinding their powerful pharyngeal or throat teeth together, using their swim bladder as a resonating organ to amplify the sounds. They also make peculiar threatening gestures, which may be a courtship ritual or a territorial display. Two Grunts of the same kind will often place themselves opposite each other as if "kissing" with their wide-open mouths showing bright orange-red inside.

Grunts are appealing fish which are quite easy to keep in the aquarium, since they accept all kinds of animal food.

FAMILY: Pomadasyidae.
SCIENTIFIC NAME: *Anisotremus virginicus* (Linnaeus).
POPULAR NAME: **Porkfish.**
DISTRIBUTION: Tropical western Atlantic Ocean from Bermuda and Florida to Brazil.
HABITAT: Reef areas.
DESCRIPTION: Cheerful coloration, especially the adult fish. Young fish have a whitish body with two black stripes and a black spot at the base of the caudal fin; the head and caudal fin are yellow. Older fish have a black band from the mouth through the eye to the nape and a second black vertical band in front of the pectoral fin. Alternate silver blue and yellow stripes run lengthwise

Porkfish

behind this second band. The fins are yellow. Very hardy. Only occasionally imported.
LENGTH: To 30 cm (12 inches).
COMMENT: Fry have been observed as cleaners (see page 94). Younger fish somewhat cranky.

French Grunt

FAMILY: Pomadasyidae.

SCIENTIFIC NAME: *Haemulon flavolineatum* (Demarest).

POPULAR NAME: **French Grunt.**

DISTRIBUTION: Tropical western Atlantic Ocean from Virginia to Rio de Janeiro.

HABITAT: Reef areas.

DESCRIPTION: Somewhat varying coloration: body is usually bluish silver with yellow stripes. The stripes below the lateral line are oblique, those above are horizontal. Fins are yellowish. Very hardy.

LENGTH: To 30 cm (12 inches).

CARE: When possible, should be kept in a small group. Not demanding in regard to food.

CROAKERS AND DRUMS

Croakers are shallows dwellers in tropical and sub-tropical seas. Some members of the family (Sciaenidae) are known to utter sounds, which arise from muscle pressure on the swim bladder (hence also called "Drum"). Typical of many species is the narrow, lengthened, frontal dorsal fin, which is often hardly connected to the lower and longer dorsal fin. The mouth is usually powerful and rounded off.

Croakers feed on animal food. They require a great deal of open swimming space and like a sandy bottom. They are sensitive to skin damage.

FAMILY: Sciaenidae.
SCIENTIFIC NAME: *Equetus acuminatus* (Bloch and Schneider).
POPULAR NAME: **Cubbyu; High Hat.**
DISTRIBUTION: Tropical western Atlantic Ocean, Caribbean Sea as far north as Florida.
HABITAT: Found around rocks and reefs close to shore, sometimes in inland bays. Often in groups beneath rock ledges in daytime.
DESCRIPTION: Alternating dark brown to black and white longitudinal stripes. The dark stripes are alternately narrow and broad. The dorsal fin is

Cubbyu; High Hat

dark brown or black with a light edge. As the fish grows, the high, frontal dorsal fin becomes smaller in proportion to the rest of the body. Old fish tend to be disagreeable.

LENGTH: To 25 cm (10 inches).

CARE: A rather hardy species which, however, requires close attention. It is a slow eater, and fond of shrimp.

FAMILY: Sciaenidae.
SCIENTIFIC NAME: *Equetus lanceolatus* (Linnaeus).
POPULAR NAME: **Jackknife; Ribbon Fish.**
DISTRIBUTION: Tropical western Atlantic Ocean and the Caribbean Sea.
HABITAT: Prefers deeper water than Cubbyu.
DESCRIPTION: Grey with 3 white-edged bands of dark brown or black. One of these runs vertically through the eye, another from the nape to the pelvis, and the third from the first dorsal fin to the end of the caudal fin. Not very hardy and rather shy.
LENGTH: To 25 cm (10 inches).
CARE: When first placed in the aquarium, it must be fed live crabs.
COMMENT: Extraordinarily sensitive to being transported.

Jackknife; Ribbon Fish

SNAPPERS

This predatory family (Lutjanidae) of Perch-like fishes, which is widespread in tropical seas, is comprised of fast-growing school fishes. Adults usually live as loners.

Snappers are slim, high-backed species which are good for the aquarium, as long as they are not kept with small fishes, which easily fall prey to them. Generally, they are meat eaters with sharp teeth.

Be sure to provide adequate swimming room and sufficient hiding places.

FAMILY: Lutjanidae.
SCIENTIFIC NAME: *Lutjanus kasmira* (Forskäl).
POPULAR NAME: **Blue-striped Snapper.**
DISTRIBUTION: Tropical Indo-Pacific region.
HABITAT: Offshore waters.
DESCRIPTION: Yellowish brown above, becoming yellowish white towards the lower sides. Four or five bright blue, black-edged bands run the length of the body and onto the head. The fins are yellowish to yellowish red. Keeps the same pattern when grown, but is more vibrant. Very hardy and rather peaceful. Only occasionally imported.
LENGTH: To 40 cm (16 inches).

Occasionally found on the market are: *Lutjanus apodus, L. decussatus, L. fulviflamma, L. sanguineus.*

Blue-striped Snapper

FAMILY: Lutjanidae.
SCIENTIFIC NAME: *Lutjanus sebae* (Cuvier and Valenciennes).
POPULAR NAME: **Red Emperor.**
DISTRIBUTION: Tropical Indo-Pacific region.
HABITAT: Offshore waters.
DESCRIPTION: Young fish are very attractive with three broad, reddish-brown bands, which later turn a washed-out, muddy red. Grows extraordinarily rapidly. Occasionally imported individually.
LENGTH: To 1 m ($39\frac{1}{4}$ inches).
CARE: A voracious eater; do not overfeed fry.

SQUIRREL FISHES AND SOLDIER FISHES

Squirrel Fishes, twilight and night-time predatory members of the Holocentridae family, are usually red and have big, bulging eyes, a stiff spine at the beginning of the anal fin, and rough scales. (Because their eyes are sensitive, do not use a net to catch them.) They are found in all tropical seas, on reefs and in the shallows.

In the aquarium, Squirrel Fishes are relatively easy to care for, but, because of their size, they must have a tank that provides adequate room. They require many hiding places in the aquarium and like to lurk under overhangs, where they can attack their prey with lightning speed.

In the beginning, you may have difficulty getting your Squirrel Fish to eat. Offer it live crabs or small fish. Later on, it will eat all kinds of animal food. Squirrel Fishes consider all small fish as legitimate prey.

FAMILY: Holocentridae.

SCIENTIFIC NAME: *Holocentrus ruber* Bennett.

POPULAR NAME: **Red-striped Soldier Fish; Red-striped Squirrel Fish.**

DISTRIBUTION: Widespread in tropical Indo-Pacific waters up to Japan; also found in the Red Sea, through the Suez Canal, and as far as the coasts of Israel and Lebanon.

HABITAT: Shallow reef areas.

DESCRIPTION: The body is red with 8 whitish longitudinal bands. The upper membrane between the dorsal spines is blackish, as is the area between the third and fourth anal spines and the first soft anal ray. There are also dark streaks on the edge of the ventral fin and the upper and lower caudal lobes. Very hardy.

LENGTH: To 20 cm (8 inches).

COMMENT: This is the most frequently imported Squirrel Fish species. Utters sounds. Recommended.

Related species also imported are: *Holocentrus ascensionis, H. diadema, H. spinifer* and *H. xantherythrus.*

Red-striped Squirrel Fish

FAMILY: Holocentridae.

SCIENTIFIC NAME: *Myripristis jacobus* Cuvier and Valenciennes.

POPULAR NAME: **Black-bar Soldier Fish; Black-bar Squirrel Fish.**

DISTRIBUTION: Widespread in the Caribbean area.

HABITAT: Coral reefs.

DESCRIPTION: Red flattened body with striking black eyes and a black bar just behind the gills. Very hardy. Not regularly imported.

LENGTH: To 20 cm (8 inches); smaller in the aquarium.

CARE: This fish feels better in a group. Prefers brine shrimp, guppies, earthworms, and other live foods.

Other related species are *Myripristis adustus* and *M. murdjan*, from the Indo-Pacific region, whose spawning activity at the water surface has been observed.

Black-bar Soldier Fish

SEA BASS, GROUPERS, AND ROCK COD

Most of the 400 known species of this family (Serranidae) are large predatory fishes found on rocky coasts and reefs, usually in the tropics, but sometimes in temperate zones. Most of the species are reserved for exhibition tanks, and only a few remain small enough to be suitable for the amateur. Lengths from 3 cm ($1\frac{1}{8}$ inches) to over 3 m (10 feet) are possible.

Most of the species are quite hardy in the aquarium and are not very demanding in regard to food and water quality. Hybrids among them are capable of reproduction. Because of their predatory tendencies (they attack their prey from under cover), Sea Bass and Groupers should only be kept in the same tank with larger fishes, or those of equal size.

Even a beginner can derive a great deal of pleasure from these magnificent fish, if care is taken in selecting their tank companions. They are easily "domesticated" and even learn to recognize their keeper.

Serranids are easy to feed with the flesh of fish, mussels or beef heart. They also accept large shrimp.

Panther Fish; Polka-dot Grouper

FAMILY: Serranidae.
SCIENTIFIC NAME: *Chromileptis altivelis* (Cuvier and Valenciennes).
POPULAR NAME: **Panther Fish; Polka-dot Grouper.**
DISTRIBUTION: Indian Ocean to the western Pacific.
HABITAT: Rock and reef areas.
DESCRIPTION: The body and head are greyish, becoming lighter on the abdomen. The fins are grey. The body is entirely covered with round, black, white-edged spots, the largest of which lie

on the head, central body and dorsal fin. The number and size of these spots vary with the age and size of the specimen; there are proportionately fewer in larger fish. Very hardy. Imported individually relatively regularly.
LENGTH: To 50 cm (20 inches); usually smaller in the aquarium.
CARE: Keep with fish of its own size or larger. Relatively peaceful, but requires considerable swimming room and many hiding places.
COMMENT: This fish has a small head and large pectoral fins, and does not grow too rapidly. A recommended species, since the small mouth confines it to relatively small prey.

FAMILY: Serranidae.
SCIENTIFIC NAME: *Diploprion bifasciatum* Cuvier and Valenciennes.
POPULAR NAME: **Double-banded Sea Perch.**
DISTRIBUTION: Indian Ocean to the Sunda Sea of Indonesia.
HABITAT: Reef areas.
DESCRIPTION: The body is yellowish with two dark or black cross bands. One runs through the eye; the other, much broader band, covers the posterior half of the body. The head is sometimes brownish yellow. Rarely hides. Can overpower fish up to its own size. Imported individually only.
LENGTH: To 24 cm (9½ inches).

Double-banded Sea Perch

CARE: For good health, requires live, small crabs. When frightened, gives off a whitish skin secretion from the entire body surface which can be fatal to other fish. Take care in handling!

Similar suitable members of the family Serranidae which are occasionally imported are: *Epinephelus flavocaeruleus*, *E. caeruleopunctatus*, *Cephalopholis argus*, *Hypoplectrus* species, *Diplectrum* species and *Serranus* species.

Blue-spot Rock Cod; Jewel Bass

FAMILY: Serranidae.
SCIENTIFIC NAME: *Cephalopholis miniatus* (Forskäl).
POPULAR NAME: **Blue-spot Rock Cod; Jewel Bass.**
DISTRIBUTION: Tropical Indo-Pacific region.
HABITAT: Coastal waters.
DESCRIPTION: One of the most beautiful species. Red to reddish brown, usually, but not always, with darker vertical bands. The head, body and all the fins are covered with numerous small blue spots. The dorsal, anal and caudal fins have a fine white border. Imported individually only.
LENGTH: To 45 cm (18 inches).
CARE: In the aquarium, this fish hides all the time; provide open caves to keep it in view. Somewhat particular about its food; prefers shrimp and mussels.

FAMILY: Serranidae.
SCIENTIFIC NAME: *Grammistes sexlineatus* (Thunberg).
POPULAR NAME: **Golden-striped Grouper; Six-lined Grouper.**
DISTRIBUTION: Tropical Indo-Pacific region.
HABITAT: Reef areas.
DESCRIPTION: The body is a deep chestnut brown with several milk white to golden longitudinal stripes. The number of stripes increases with age from 3 to as many as 9. Infrequently imported. Very hardy (have been kept for more than ten years).
LENGTH: To 25 cm (10 inches).
CARE: Swims a great deal in open water; keep only with fish that are at least the same size.
COMMENT: When excited (for example, at being caught), discharges a black, poisonous excretion from the anal gland which can kill other fish. Beware!

SEA HORSES AND PIPE FISHES

The upright Sea Horse and the long, thin and extended Pipe Fish (family Syngnathidae) both have heavily ossified skin and reduced caudal fins. They swim with their dorsal and pectoral fins. Sea Horses must have places they can grip with their prehensile tail, as well as adequate swimming room.

Sea Horses and Pipe Fishes exhibit interesting mating and brood care. The female Pipe Fish adheres the eggs to the underbelly of the male who, depending on the species, constructs a specifically shaped brood fold to receive and incubate the eggs. "Carrying time" varies from 10 days to 1½ months. Young Sea Horses can be reared on ciliates *(Euplotes)*, and many on *Artemia nauplius* (a crustacean larva), which must be carefully separated from the egg shells. Sea Horses grow very rapidly, approaching adulthood in half a year.

Neither Sea Horses nor Pipe Fishes are very demanding in regard to water quality, but they are absolute plankton eaters that are very difficult to acclimatize to artificial food. Live food is important. Recommended are live *Mysis* and the larger *Artemia*, white and black gnat larvae, large *Daphnia* and *Cyclops*. Many syngnathids also accept young guppies. They will probably also eat frozen food as long as it floats and is aerated with large air bubbles. They approach food warily, then suddenly suck it into their tubular mouths. It is best to keep syngnathids separately with their own family, or with very calm fish with similar eating habits.

In the Wilhelma Aquarium in Stuttgart, Germany, *Hippocampus kuda* was kept into the fifth generation and a Philippine variety to the fourth. Sea Horses live to be barely over 3 years old. Once the food problem has been solved, keeping them is easy and rewarding.

FAMILY: Syngnathidae.

SCIENTIFIC NAME: *Dunckerocampus dactyliophorus* (Bleeker).

POPULAR NAME: **Zebra Pipe Fish.**

DISTRIBUTION: Indonesian-Australian Archipelago.

HABITAT: Coastal waters.

DESCRIPTION: Head and body are encircled by black to brown rings, sometimes edged with white. The caudal fin is red with a white rim. The male shown in the illustration is burdened with eggs. Only occasionally imported.

LENGTH: To 15 cm (6 inches).

CARE: Requires small, soft-shelled, live food, such as immature *Artemia*.

Zebra
Pipe Fish

Oceanic Sea Horse

FAMILY: Syngnathidae.
SCIENTIFIC NAME: *Hippocampus kuda.*
POPULAR NAME: **Oceanic Sea Horse.**
DISTRIBUTION: Tropical Indo-Pacific region.
HABITAT: Coastal waters.
DESCRIPTION: Brownish to yellowish olive becoming a yellowish white on the ventral side; sometimes brownish black with orange undertones or golden yellow. One of the largest species in this family and probably the easiest to keep. Regularly imported.
LENGTH: To 20 cm (8 inches).
COMMENT: Just as easy to keep is the Pygmy Sea Horse, *Hippocampus zosterae,* which has a life expectancy of about a year and is easy to rear.

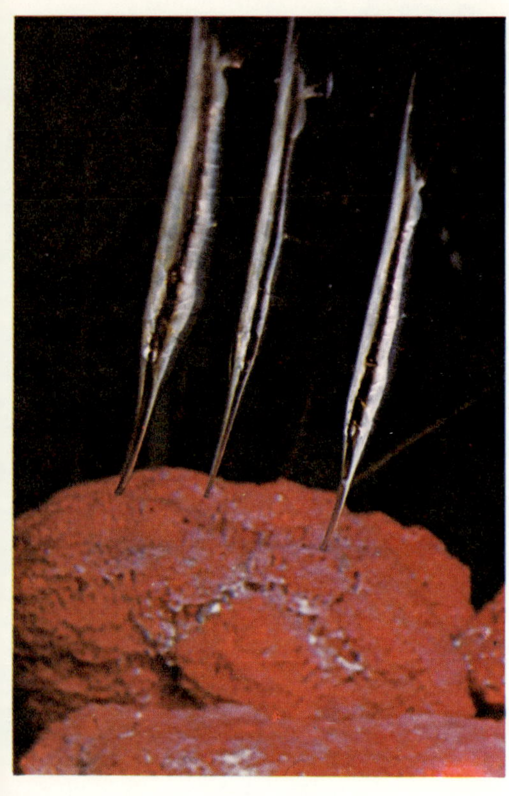

Razor Fish;
Shrimpfish

FAMILY: Centriscidae.
SCIENTIFIC NAME: *Aeoliscus strigatus* (Günther).
POPULAR NAME: **Razor Fish; Shrimpfish.**
DISTRIBUTION: Indian and Pacific Oceans.
HABITAT: Shallow water.
DESCRIPTION: Related to the Sea Horse, this fish swims standing on its head. Its compressed, knife-like body is covered with armoured plates and has a very sharp edge along the belly and vertical fins, all of which are placed at the end of the body. It lives in schools, and swims in co-ordinated movements. Only occasionally imported.
LENGTH: To about 15 cm (6 inches).
CARE: With its tubular mouth, it can take in only very small live food: *Daphnia, Cyclops, Artemia,* and small *Mysis*. With the correct food, it can be kept for years and will be very rewarding. Should be kept only with similar soft-food eaters.

FAMILY: Opistognathidae.
SCIENTIFIC NAME: *Opistognathus aurifrons* (Jordan and Thompson).
POPULAR NAME: **Yellowhead Jawfish.**
DISTRIBUTION: Caribbean Sea.
HABITAT: Bottom dweller in fairly shallow waters.
DESCRIPTION: Light bluish-grey body with numerous pale blue dots. The head to the dorsal fin is yellow. Has small scales, strong jaws, and large moveable eyes. Constructs caves for itself, which it guards and is a mouth breeder. Very hardy. Found regularly in Caribbean imports.
LENGTH: To 12 cm ($4\frac{3}{4}$ inches).
CARE: Likes small, live food. Inclined towards ulceration of the throat region when iodine is lacking.

Yellowhead
Jawfish

MORAY EELS

Tropical seas yield some exceedingly interesting species of the Moray Eel (Muraenidae), which at last have found their way into amateur aquariums, even though they are twilight and night-time creatures. Species that remain small are best suited for the aquarium, as they can be kept with other fishes that are not too small.

You must provide caves in the aquarium into which Moray Eels can withdraw as much as possible, if not entirely. Many species bury themselves in sand. Make sure that the aquarium is tightly covered, since Moray Eels find every crack and will jump out.

Many Moray Eels accept all kinds of substitute animal food, such as pieces of shrimp or fish, but others are very particular and hard to acclimatize. Once you have found a suitable food, you can keep Moray Eels for years.

Beware of being bitten by a Moray, for the bite can lead to infection.

FAMILY: Muraenidae.
SCIENTIFIC NAME: *Echidna zebra* (Shaw).
POPULAR NAME: **Zebra Moray.**
DISTRIBUTION: Tropical Indo-Pacific region.
HABITAT: Shore and reef areas.
DESCRIPTION: Dark reddish or purplish brown, with 30 to more than 100 narrow white, pale yellow or

Zebra Moray

golden rings, each bordered by an edge darker than the ground. The tail is short and just as thick as the body. Very hardy. Imported individually somewhat regularly.

LENGTH: To 120 cm (about 4 feet).

CARE: The Zebra Moray eats only shrimp, and has not yet been persuaded to partake of any other food.

Snowflake Moray Eel

FAMILY: Muraenidae.
SCIENTIFIC NAME: *Echidna nebulosa* (Ahl).
POPULAR NAME: **Snowflake Moray Eel.**
DISTRIBUTION: Widespread in the tropical Indo-Pacific from the Red Sea to the Philippines and Australia.
HABITAT: Reef and shore areas; small fish are sometimes found in tidepools.
DESCRIPTION: Yellowish, brownish or whitish, but sometimes a rich dark brown. Two rows of large, black, starlike or amoeba-shaped spots run lengthwise along the back and the lower part of the body. Each of these large spots contains 1 to 3 smaller white or yellow spots. The lower spots are connected by black bands which cross the underside of the body. The spaces between the larger spots are thickly sprinkled with fine irregular lines and spots. The coloration increases with growth. Very hardy. Often imported.
LENGTH: To 1.5 m (about 5 feet); usually much smaller.
CARE: Not particular about food.
COMMENT: Although it is a relatively peaceful species, it is feared by native fishermen in some regions as a fierce and savage biter. Recommended for the aquarium.

FAMILY: Muraenidae.
SCIENTIFIC NAME: *Rhinomuraena amboinensis* (Bleeker).
POPULAR NAME: **Blue Ribbon Eel; Ghost Moray; Hare Moray.**
DISTRIBUTION: Eastern Sunda Sea, Indonesia, and the Philippines.
HABITAT: Reef areas.
DESCRIPTION: Attractive and not very aggressive. Gleaming blue of the imported fish usually darkens later. More frequently imported recently.
LENGTH: To 90 cm (36 inches).
CARE: Very sensitive towards acclimatization. Prefers to eat the flesh of fish. Otherwise very hardy and easy to keep.

Blue Ribbon Eel; Ghost Moray

FAMILY: Plotosidae.
SCIENTIFIC NAME: *Plotosus anguillaris* (Bloch).
POPULAR NAME: **Barber; Coral Catfish; Eel Catfish; Salt-water Catfish; Striped Catfish.**
DISTRIBUTION: Widespread in the Indo-Pacific region.
HABITAT: Found in reef, shore and estuarial waters.
DESCRIPTION: Drab grey to chestnut brown or black. Young fish have two or three bright yellow to white lengthwise stripes from the tip of the head to the tail. These fade somewhat with age. There are four pairs of barbels on the chin and a peculiar, tree-like appendage attached behind the vent, the purpose of which is unknown. Very hardy. Only this single species of Catfish is regularly imported.
LENGTH: 25 to 30 cm (10 to 12 inches).
CARE: Willingly accepts almost every kind of animal food; give the fry time to eat. Accompany it in the tank with larger fishes.
COMMENT: The Barber is a school fish and should be kept as such. The fry, especially, make their school into a "rolling ball" along the bottom.

Caution: These fish carry venom on the pectoral spines and are capable of inflicting painful and even dangerous wounds. They are feared and respected by native fishermen.

Barber; Salt-water Catfish

SCORPION FISHES

Scorpion Fishes (Scorpaenidae) are the only living bottom-feeding fishes found in every sea of the world. They are well camouflaged, large-headed, predatory fishes with many skin appendages and large fins. Many have poisonous spines.

One sub-family consists of the Lion Fishes (Pteroinae), which often float freely or against rock walls in the water as they wait for their living prey. Scorpion and Lion Fishes are truly magnificent in shape and coloration and often have especially long pectoral fin rays and a high, spiny dorsal fin, whose rays are poisonous. Wounds from these rays can be dangerous to humans. The poison is comparable to that of the cobra and, therefore, you should have the proper anti-toxin serum available. In all instances (in Europe) where the keeper was wounded by this fish, the wounds were terribly painful but not serious or could be treated through the circulatory system. Antivenin was also used, but its effectiveness has not been proven. It is better to take the proper precautions!

Lion and Scorpion Fishes, easy to care for in the aquarium, require live food at first, but become easily domesticated and then accept dead food, including mussel meat, pieces of shrimp and fish. If you feed them in the daytime, then the activity of this normally twilight-active fish will also be shifted to the daylight hours.

Do not keep Lion and Scorpion Fishes in the same tank with small fishes; they are peaceful towards fishes of their own size. Provide open caves or structures in the tank so they have suitable lurking places.

Accompanied by a few precautions, these fishes may be recommended for the beginning amateur, since keeping them is relatively easy.

FAMILY: Scorpaenidae.
SCIENTIFIC NAME: *Dendrochirus brachypterus* (Cuvier).
POPULAR NAME: **Dwarf Lion Fish.**

DISTRIBUTION: Indian Ocean, western Pacific and the Red Sea.
HABITAT: Coral reefs.
DESCRIPTION: A rosy body with two dark cross bands, one beneath the eye, the other over the nape. The rest of the body is more or less encircled by six broad dark cross bands. The two sets of pectoral fins are barred with black and white. The anal and caudal fins are spotted with rows of black spots. This is the smallest of the Lion Fishes. Very hardy. Regularly imported.
LENGTH: To 17 cm (6¾ inches).
CARE: Keep in the same way as other Lion Fishes. This fish can become accustomed to dead food.
COMMENT: A very similar and equally hardy species is *Dendrochirus zebra*.

Caution: As with all Scorpion Fishes, handle with extreme care.

FAMILY: Scorpaenidae.
SCIENTIFIC NAME: *Dendrochirus zebra* Quoy and Gaimard.
POPULAR NAME: **Spotfin Lion Fish.**
DISTRIBUTION: Indian Ocean to the central Pacific; occasionally found in brackish water.
HABITAT: Shallow reef areas.
DESCRIPTION: More or less red or rose red with reddish-black cross bands. There are 2 or 3 bands on the head and 6 or 7 on the trunk of the body.

Spotfin Lion Fish

Some of the pectoral rays are branched at the ends. Very hardy. Regularly imported.

LENGTH: To 20 cm (8 inches).

CARE: Easily acclimatized, it can be accustomed to dead food.

COMMENT: A similar species, *Pterois antennata*, is distinguished by its unbranched and thread-like pectoral rays which reach back or beyond the caudal fin.

Caution: Dorsal and anal spines are venomous.

FAMILY: Scorpaenidae.

SCIENTIFIC NAME: *Pterois radiata* Cuvier and Valenciennes.

POPULAR NAME: **Whitefin Lion Fish.**

DISTRIBUTION: Indian and Pacific Oceans and the Red Sea.

HABITAT: Reef areas.

DESCRIPTION: Eight or more deep brown or red-brown bands edged in white run vertically down the body at irregular intervals, beginning at the eye. This fish is easily distinguished by the two narrow, white bars which run horizontally on the caudal base. Loose spines gleam white when the fish is excited, pink when in repose. Imported individually relatively regularly.

LENGTH: To 20 cm (8 inches).

CARE: Easy to care for; becomes accustomed reluctantly to dead food.

Whitefin Lion Fish

Butterfly Cod; Lion Fish;
Scorpion Fish; Turkey Fish

FAMILY: Scorpaenidae.

SCIENTIFIC NAME: *Pterois volitans* (Linnaeus).

POPULAR NAME: **Butterfly Cod; Lion Fish; Scorpion Fish; Turkey Fish.**

DISTRIBUTION: Widespread in the Indian and Pacific Oceans and the Red Sea.

HABITAT: Coral reefs.

DESCRIPTION: The largest species in the family with the biggest fins. The fins become smaller in proportion to the body in the course of growth. Dusky red head and body with numerous dark red or black transverse bars and stripes, bordered by white lines. The soft dorsal, anal and caudal fins have rows of dark brown or black spots. The spots on the pectoral and ventral fins are larger. Grows very rapidly. Frequently and regularly imported.

LENGTH: To 35 cm (13¾ inches).

CARE: Easy to care for; becomes accustomed to dead food.

Caution: Dorsal spines are extremely venomous.

Stonefish

FAMILY: Scorpaenidae.
SCIENTIFIC NAME: *Synanceja verrucosa* Bloch and Schneider.
POPULAR NAME: **Stonefish.**
DISTRIBUTION: Tropical Indo-Pacific region.
HABITAT: Found on coral reefs and shallow, rocky, muddy port areas and estuaries.
DESCRIPTION: Well-named as it can hardly be distinguished from its natural surroundings; a master of camouflage. Has poison glands at the base of the dorsal spines; may be considered the most poisonous of the venomous fishes. Buries itself partly in the sand, using its pectoral fins, the rest of its body being covered with many appendages and often overgrown with algae. Background coloration changes according to conditions. Only the pupil of the eye is distinguishable. Only occasionally imported.
LENGTH: To 30 cm (12 inches).
CARE: Not always easy to accustom to a change of food. After acclimatization, however, quite hardy.
COMMENT: Not a fish for the aquarist; it hardly moves, but eats other fishes, even those of its own size.

Caution: This is the most venomous of marine fishes. Death often follows a venom injection.

Sailfin Leaf Fish

FAMILY: Scorpaenidae.
SCIENTIFIC NAME: *Taenionotus triacanthus* Lacépède.
POPULAR NAME: **Sailfin Leaf Fish.**
DISTRIBUTION: Tropical Indo-Pacific region.
HABITAT: Among seaweed.
DESCRIPTION: Brown to yellowish. Leaf-shaped in side view, the body is flattened vertically with a high dorsal fin. Lives among seaweed and waves with movements of its fins. When excited, it steps up its waving or rocking movements. Only occasionally imported.
LENGTH: 15 cm (6 inches).
CARE: Delicate. Accepts practically nothing but live food, yet it is interesting and worthwhile. Do not keep with rapid eaters or very small fish. In spite of the thinness of its body, it can occasionally swallow very large bits of food.
COMMENT: It can cast off its skin entirely, thus freeing itself of algae and parasites.

FROGFISHES OR ANGLER FISHES

This is a very specialized family (Antennariidae) of bottom-feeding fishes with pectoral fins that also serve as walking organs; the ventral fins are also used in forward movement. Large gill openings, with a smaller opening at the base of the pectoral fins, are used for swimming backwards. The frontal ray of the dorsal fin is moveable and has a flap of skin on the end which is used for "angling". This flap of skin is used as bait, since it is often quite worm-like and can be jiggled up and down enticingly. When a smaller fish strikes at this bait, it is engulfed by the Angler. Many similar, unmistakable species are found in all tropical waters.

Frogfishes are calmly lurking, predatory creatures which seize their prey quite rapidly by suction and snapping. They can even overcome fish that are larger than themselves. In spite of their interesting appearance and living habits, however, Frogfishes are not recommended for the aquarium. They can hardly be acclimatized to associate with other fish and cannot be kept for a very long time.

The spawn is a long (70-cm or 28-inch), gelatinous streamer, containing about 10,000 eggs.

Eyespot Frogfish

FAMILY: Antennariidae.
SCIENTIFIC NAME: *Antennarius ocellatus* (Bloch and Schneider).
POPULAR NAME: **Eyespot Frogfish; Ocellated Angler.**
DISTRIBUTION: Caribbean Sea as far north as Florida.
HABITAT: Reefs and shallow water.
DESCRIPTION: Brown marbled with lighter brownish yellow and scattered black dots. Each side has three large black spots ocellated with brown rings:

one is on the dorsal fin near the base; another is below the first on the side of the body; the third is in the middle of the caudal fin. Young fish have considerably more coloration (pink markings which later vanish). Seldom imported.
LENGTH: To 35 cm (13¾ inches).
CARE: Very sensitive. In general, only live food is accepted.
COMMENT: About 45 Frogfish species are known; individual specimens are occasionally imported. All are somewhat the same in handling.

FAMILY: Antennariidae.
SCIENTIFIC NAME: *Histrio histrio* (Linnaeus).
POPULAR NAME: **Frogfish; Sargassum Fish.**
DISTRIBUTION: All warm seas; especially in the drifting seaweed fields of the Sargasso Sea; off South America.
HABITAT: In fields of seaweed; also occurs on reefs.
DESCRIPTION: Yellowish to cream, mottled with red, brown and black to match the Sargassum weed. It is an exceptionally well camouflaged fish; numerous bizarre, fleshy appendages over the body make it scarcely visible in its natural environment. The thin angling organ (see page 246) is hardly ever used.
LENGTH: To 15 cm (6 inches).
CARE: A very sensitive species. Although it accepts food, it cannot be kept for very long as it soon dies of unknown causes.

Frogfish; Sargassum Fish

SCIENTIFIC NAME INDEX

INDEX

PICTURE CREDITS

The publisher thanks the following for photographs and drawings used in this book: H. R. Axelrod; E. A. Baumbach; H. Burkhardt; H. Feucht; U. Friese; H. Hansen; H. Kacher; B. Kahl; K. Knaack; E. Krüger; J. Maier; W. Neugebauer; K. Paysan; W. Schmidt; H. Schrempp; H. Voigtmann; and H. W. Wolf.